PRESENCE THROUGH THE WORD

(A Scriptural Approach to the Mystery of Grace)

Sister Evelyn Ann Schumacher, O.S.F.

LIVING FLAME PRESS

Cover: Robert Manning

Copyright © 1983: Sister Evelyn Ann Schumacher, O.S.F.

ISBN: 0-914544-46-2

Published by: Living Flame Press, Box 74, Locust Valley, New York 11560.

Printed in the United States of America.

Dedication

To all the members
of my religious community —
The Franciscan Sisters of Christian Charity
Manitowoc, Wisconsin

Acknowledgments

Deep gratitude to Father George Maloney, S.J., whose prayerful support and guidance made this book possible.

Deep gratitude, likewise, to those Sisters who read the manuscript and offered many helpful suggestions.

Grateful acknowledgement to the following publishers for excerpts from *The Jerusalem Bible*, copyright 1966 by Darton, Longman & Todd, Ltd. and Doubleday & Company, Inc. Used by permission of the publisher.

Foreword

This is a book about love. It is a biblical approach to the mystery of God's Gift of Himself to us in grace. The sacred writers reveal that in the order of nature God is present in all created reality. But in the order of grace, we become one with Him in the intimacy of love. Divine revelation assures us that God's eternal plan in creating the universe is to give not merely created gifts, wonderful though they may be, but to give us the Gift of Himself.

That God is a community of three divine Persons is the fundamental doctrine of Christianity. All other teachings flow from this one truth. Ordinarily, Christians have little difficulty in accepting biblical revelation and Church teaching regarding the mystery of the Trinity. In a familiar way they address these three Persons in prayer, calling them by their personal names: the Father, the Son and the Holy Spirit. Yet, it seems that many Christians tend to think of God as some wonderful but abstract Being far beyond the realm of human relationship and the reach of human possession. Too many are under the impression that a personal intimacy with the Father, the Son and the Holy Spirit is reserved for only a few and cannot be for them.

This book deals with God's Self-Communication to us in the mystery of grace. The content is drawn mainly from Scripture and the teachings of the Eastern Christian Fathers of the Church. In formulating their doctrine on grace these illustrious Fathers drew directly from Scripture. They developed a theology of *Presence Through the Word* which is both enlightening and enriching.

In the writing of this book I found the following sources invaluable: *The Jerusalem Bible* and *The New American Bible* as well as *The Jerome Biblical Commentary* and *The Interpreter's One-Volume Commentary on the Bible*. I also had frequent recourse to the excellent scholarship found in the *Dictionary of Biblical Theology* as well as in the *Dictionary of the Bible* by John L. McKenzie, S.J.

I have endeavored to present some of the teachings of the Greek Fathers on grace. In doing so, I depended entirely on the comprehensive and masterful writings of George A. Maloney, S.J., the well-known Scripture and patristic scholar and recognized authority on Eastern Christian Spirituality.

While I realize that this book is a simple and limited approach to the profound mystery of grace, I pray that it will be of some value to those who read it. It is my hope that it will be a means of bringing the reader to a more conscious awareness of God's loving presence deep within each one's own heart.

— Sister Evelyn Ann Schumacher, O.S.F.
January 28, 1983
Feast of St. Thomas Aquinas

Table of Contents

Introduction

The Eastern Christian Fathers of the Church drew from both the Old and New Testaments in the development of their doctrine on grace. These Fathers are known for their humble and prayerful approach to the Word of God. Their teachings, therefore, have a distinctive quality and richness because they theologized out of Scripture and the mystical experiences they were given in their prayerful listening to God's Word.

In their doctrine on grace the eastern theologians saw the need to make a distinction between the essence of God and His uncreated energies of love. They taught that God is unknowable and inaccessible in His essence; yet, He does communicate Himself to created reality in His uncreated energies of love. Therefore, God does have real existence in the world, for the energies

11

of His love are inseparable from Himself.

According to the Fathers, the energies of God's love are not "things" or "gifts" apart from Himself. They are His Wisdom, His pre-existing Word, His eternal thought-life which flows unceasingly out of the depths of His inner life of love. Just as we ourselves are present in the thoughts we speak, so is God present in the thoughts He speaks. Grace, then, is primarily not something created, but it is God communicating Himself to us in the uncreated energies of His love through the power of the Holy Spirt and His blessed Son, the Word-Made-Flesh.

Image and Likeness

The Eastern Fathers built their theology of grace on the biblical concept of image and likeness. In the biblical account of the creation of Adam, the sacred writer reveals the desire and loving plan of God to communicate His own Spirit of Love to a creature who would resemble Him:

Let us make man in our image,
in the likeness of ourselves . . . (Genesis 2:26).

When God breathed the Spirit of His love into the nostrils of Adam, He gave him more than mere natural life. He gave him the power to give love and to receive love. In doing so, God put into human nature potential for His own divine Being. Since love is something that cannot be forced, but must be given knowingly and willingly, God gave to Adam an intellect and a free will.

In the early days of his existence, Adam was in complete control of all the powers of his richly gifted nature. He was deeply conscious of God's love for him and he was happy and secure in this knowledge. In his expanding consciousness of God and of all creatures, he grew in greater likeness to God.

As long as Adam was attentive to God's presence and remained open to receive the divine thoughts the Spirit was communicating to him, evil could not enter his life. But when he deliberately chose to believe a "lie" in preference to the truth he was receiving from God, Adam broke the flow of communication between himself and his Creator. He did not lose his potential for God but he did lose his capacity to grow in likeness to Him. Sin is the misuse of human freedom. It impedes or hinders growth in likeness to God.

No longer able to distinguish truth from falsehood, Adam's life took on unholy characteristics and he alienated himself not only from God but also from other people. Human love would have

13

to be liberated from its unholy tendencies. This was to become the task of Jesus Christ, the Word-Made-Flesh.

The Word of God

Love is the longing to share our presence with others. It is the longing to share not only physical proximity, but also our inner selves. Ordinarily, we do this by externalizing the thoughts and feelings hidden within us through the words that we speak or write. Hence, it can be said that our unexpressed words pre-exist in the thoughts we think. In manifesting our thoughts, we externalize the spirit of our love which can influence the lives of others in one way or another.

Since love is God's essential energy, He seeks to share His Inner Self beyond the Godhead. His Almighty Word pre-exists in His sublime, unchangeable and holy thoughts eternally. In the act of creating, God sent forth the energies of His creative and life-giving Spirit of Love by speaking His All-Powerful Word. He thus brought the universe into existence.

In the prologue to the fourth gospel, St. John identifies the pre-existing Word, sometimes called the Logos of God, with God Himself:

14

> *In the beginning was the Word:*
> *the Word was with God*
> *and the Word was God (John 1:1).*

Several lines later John announces that the Eternal Word of God took on human flesh. He sees Jesus as the pre-existing Word, the only Son of God, the perfect Self-Image of the Father Who is in full possession of all the uncreated energies of God's inner life of love:

> *The Word was made flesh,*
> *he lived among us,*
> *and we saw his glory,*
> *the glory that is his as the only Son of the*
> *Father,*
> *full of grace and truth (John 1:14).*

The Wisdom of God

In the Old Testament in particular, we find many references to the Wisdom of God. In studying the history of the Israelites we see how God progressively communicated His Wisdom to these people, especially through the Law and the prophets. In reflecting on the Old Testament Wisdom Literature, New Testament theologians began to identify the Word-Made-Flesh with the Wisdom of God present with Him before the beginning of time.

The New Testament writers found in the original presentations of Wisdom apt concepts in which they could trace the divine origin of Jesus. They noted that both Wisdom and Jesus have been beloved by God from the very beginning. Both live intimately in union with God and both share fully in the uncreated energies of His love. Like Wisdom, the Son of God also was sent forth from God. These are but a few such parallels. St. Paul speaks of God's supreme communication of Himself in Jesus Christ when he calls Him "the power and the wisdom of God" (I Corinthians 1:24).

Following the thought-pattern of the New Testament writers, the Eastern Fathers of the Church drew extensively from the Wisdom Literature in fashioning a theology of *Presence Through the Word*. They pondered long and carefully the biblical revelations on the communication of divine Wisdom.

In reflecting prayerfully on the New Testament writings, the Fathers saw in Jesus Christ a human being Who is in full possession of all the uncreated energies of God's love. They saw human fulfillment and perfection in terms of growing in likeness to Jesus, the perfect Image of the Father:

In his body lies the fullness of divinity,
  and in him you too

find your own fulfillment . . . (Colossians 2:9).

For the Fathers, growing in likeness to Christ did not mean imitating His virtues in an endeavor to take on His characteristics through our own human efforts. They did not view Jesus merely as a moral example outside of us Whom we should try to resemble. On the other hand, growing in likeness to Christ means moving into true human fulfillment. This implies nothing less than assimilation to Christ through the power of His Holy Spirit of Love.

The Spirit in Our Lives

When Adam deliberately destroyed his personal relationship to God by refusing to listen to the communications of the Holy Spirit, human "thinking" became essentially self-centered. Without being aware of it, we can very easily cultivate selfish attitudes and absorb false values. We find it difficult to confront ourselves honestly; we have trouble discerning between truth and falsehood; and, above all, we tend to think that we are unloved by God. Such are the tendencies in human nature since the time of the first sin. The "spirit" of our love depends upon our desires, thoughts, attitudes and values. Consequently, it is our thought-life hidden deep within us that controls our relationship to God, to other people and to all created reality.

In Christian Baptism God sends His own Holy Spirit of Love into our hearts. His divine intent is to re-establish communication between Himself and us, His creatures whom He has made according to His own Image and Likeness. It is the role of the Spirit to communicate to us the thoughts, attitudes and values of God Himself. But in order to receive the Word that the Spirit wishes to communicate to us, we must learn to "quiet" the turbulent and sometimes hostile thoughts which race through our minds almost unceasingly. But how do we do this?

In order to reach the inner stillness and tranquillity needed to become aware of the presence of the Spirit within us, we must take time each day to stand before God, alone and in silence. We need regular periods of silence and solitude in our lives if we wish to enter into ourselves and find God there. Over-absorption in activities makes silence and solitude most difficult and deep interior prayer next to impossible. It is the Holy Spirit Who puts us in touch with God Himself Who is present in the "thoughts" He communicates to us. Hence, inner quiet is necessary if we are to "tune in" to the Wisdom, the uncreated energies of love which come to us directly from the inner love-life of the Trinity. It is through the activity of the Spirit in our lives that our own inner thought-life is changed and our "unholy" love is made holy.

Assimilation to Christ

In His magnificent discourse the day after Jesus fed the people on the hillside, He instructed them on the nature of the Eucharist. He began His teaching on the bread which gives life by identifying Himself with the true bread from heaven. Jesus taught that He alone can satisfy our longing for human fulfillment and unending happiness:

> I am the living bread
>   which has come down from heaven.
> Anyone who eats this bread will live forever;
>   and the bread that I shall give
>   is my flesh, for the life of the world (John
>   6:51).

Jesus began to teach about the mystery of grace when He spoke of the mutual possession of life between Himself and the person who partakes of the "bread from heaven."

> He who eats my flesh
>   and drinks my blood
>   lives in me and I live in him (John 6:56).

In these awesome words Jesus heralds the Good News that the inner love-life which He shares in fullness with the Father and the Holy Spirit is available to us. Now in His glorified humanity, the risen Jesus passes on to us in the Eucharist the life of glory, power and knowledge which He receives in fullness from the Father:

> As I, who am sent by the living Father,
> myself draw life from the Father,
> so whoever eats me
> will draw life from me (John 6:57).

However, we must remember that mutual self-giving is essential to the deepening of any relationship. We should go to the Eucharist not just to receive the Self-Gift of Another, but also to offer our own self as gift. The more we "die to self" in true metanoia and surrender our lives in humility and love to the Father in the Liturgy of the Eucharist, the more do we grow in likeness to Jesus Christ, the perfect Image of the Father. In growing in likeness to Christ, we assimilate into our own lives the "power and wisdom" which He possesses in fullness with the Father in the Spirit of Love. In this way our human thought-life is transformed and divinized. We begin to approach our daily life situations and relate to others with the thoughts, attitudes and values of Jesus Christ Himself.

Obviously, growing in likeness to Christ is more than merely imitating His virtues. It means sharing ever more consciously in the inner love-life of the Trinity. According to the Eastern Fathers, our total person (body, soul and spirit) is healed and divinized by God Himself Who comes to us directly in His uncreated energies of love through Jesus Christ and His Holy Spirit of Love. Thus, we become one with God through His Self-Communication to us in the mystery of grace.

1

The Biblical Meaning
of Heart

The connotations of the word "heart" have a much wider range in the Hebrew language than in the English. Anyone who ponders the biblical use of this word will be amazed at the many and diverse meanings the sacred writers give to it. Scripturally, the heart is the symbol of that inner "fountain" out of which flow all our affections, passions, desires and thoughts. It is that mysterious invisible "place" within us where our "spirit" meets God's Holy Spirit in the mutual self-surrender of love. It is in this meeting that we are touched and transformed in the depths of our being.

In the language of the Eastern Fathers of the Church this prayer is known as "prayer of the heart." The one word which best describes this kind of prayer is the word surrender.

Hebrew Connotations of "Heart"

In many Old Testament passages the heart is designated as the seat of intelligence. For example, to say in the heart means to think; a big heart suggests extensive knowledge; give me your heart means to give me your attention; and a hardened heart means a closed mind. One writer points out that a closed mind is remedied by the exchange of a heart of stone for a heart of flesh.

In other passages we find the heart recognized as the center of emotional activity. To cite a few examples, the heart is glad or cheerful; the heart experiences religious exultation; the heart feels grief, sadness, disappointment, vexation, worry and anguish.

In the Old Testament we find many other meanings attached to the word "heart": to reckon in the heart means to plan; to have a firm heart is the sign of courage; to steal one's heart does not mean to win someone's affections but to deceive another. Then again, Yahweh examines the heart; He alone knows the heart; God will not spurn a contrite heart; Yahweh will create a clean heart within.

The heart is also referred to many times in the New Testament. Here it is seen mainly as the place where the divine activities of God transform the Christian: the Spirit is sent into the heart of the baptized Christian, the love of God is poured into the heart through the Spirit and the Risen Christ dwells in our hearts.

Obviously both the Old and New Testaments abound with texts which reveal that our exterior behavior comes out of the desires present in our hearts. These desires more or less unconsciously find expression in our thoughts. Our thoughts may be externalized through the words we speak and the manner in which we conduct ourselves. The yearnings in our heart, then, are the source of our every thought, word and deed. The sacred writer was fully aware of this when he wrote:

> More than all else, keep watch over your heart, since here are the wellsprings of life (Proverbs 4:23).

Dispositions of the Heart

In the early days of their existence the first man and woman experienced abiding joy and peace of heart. They lived in beautiful harmony with God, with one another and with all creatures. But something happened to human nature when Adam and Eve deliberately excluded God from their lives by believing a "lie" in preference to the truth of His Word. At this point the human heart took on the capacity to be deceived:

No! You will not die!
God knows in fact
that on the day you eat it
your eyes will be opened
and you will be like gods,
knowing good and evil (Genesis 3:4-6).

This illusion about their relationship to God broke the flow of direct communication between God and Adam and Eve. In freeing themselves from all dependence on God, their hearts became so full of pride that they made themselves the criterion of good and evil.

No longer able to hear the Word of God, Adam and Eve now mistook deception for truth. No longer aware of God's unending love for them, they allowed fear, anger and hatred to enter their hearts. Adam blamed Eve and Eve blamed the serpent. The very first act of violence in human history took place when Cain killed Abel. Gone were the happy and carefree days when people lived in close communion with God and in perfect harmony with all of His creatures. The spontaneity of perfectly balanced dispositions of heart had been exchanged for the anxieties and compulsions of a nature struggling along without God. The human journey back to Him could not be made without divine intervention.

Hidden Designs of the Heart

In all of our personal relationships to God and to those with whom we live and work, the interior dispositions and attitudes in our hearts are of the greatest significance. Not only does the human heart have the dangerous capacity to be deceived and to deceive others, but it also has the incredible capacity to deceive even itself. So often we do not know our own hearts because there is so much that lies below the level of our conscious awareness.

Those deep, self-serving desires in our hearts which orient our lives in devious ways away from what is truly good and toward what is only apparently good may be quite unknown to us. We may be wholly unaware of those traits in our character which hinder intimacy with God and impede genuine and mature relationships with others. Hence, without realizing it, we may be quite out of touch with our real selves.

The heart is more devious than any other thing, perverse too: who can pierce its secrets? (Jeremiah 17:9).

While the secret designs of our hearts may be hidden from others and even from ourselves, they can never be hidden from God:

God does not see as man sees;
man looks at appearances
but Yahweh looks at the heart (1 Samuel
16:7).

Reflection

It may take courage to look into the deeper
recesses of our hearts to see what is there. But we
should not be afraid to do this, for the Holy Spirit
will help us if we ask for enlightenment. It is important that each evening before retiring, we
place ourselves in the presence of our all-loving
God and examine the underlying motivation that
worked through our thoughts, words and deeds
of the day. Only through the personal experience
of such prayerful reflection can we deepen our
level of consciousness, become aware of our real
self and come to know who we are before God.

A listening attentive heart is needed in order
to recognize any movements of selfishness that
may be in our thoughts. If these movements are
not discerned and checked, they will be externalized in our words and deeds. That is why vigi-
lance is always needed in our thought-life.

Without regular times for silence and prayerful reflection we toy with the danger of knowing
ourselves only at a superficial level. In knowing
ourselves only superficially, we run the risk of
relating to God and to other people in a more or

less superficial way.

As we grow in our understanding of the biblical meaning of heart, we gradually come to realize that the heart is the place where we meet God. The more we come to know our true self, the more do we dispose our hearts to receive the All-Powerful Word of God. It is in openness to this Word that true freedom becomes rooted in the unity of two wills: the divine and the human. It is in this union that the heart becomes a meeting place with God in an experience of love, a "meeting" which is beyond the power of human words to describe. Having found the Trinity within, we are enabled to make choices, to perform our duties and to relate to others in our daily life situations with a power that is more than merely human.

2

The Power of the Word

Love is the silent longing for presence that is found in the heart of every human being. It is the most natural thing in the world for friends to seek each other's company. How eagerly they look forward to their next meeting! But the presence they seek is far more than mere physical proximity. Friends want to make present to each other their hidden inner self which lies beyond the power of the external senses to behold, to hear or to touch. They long to make present to one another their inner world of thoughts which harbor all the joys and disappointments, the fears and frustrations, the desires and hopes that spring up unceasingly from the wellspring of their hearts.

The Human Word

In all human relationships the spoken word is the most common medium for making our hidden inner self present to others. The spoken word, however, is more than an articulation of our thoughts. Since our thought-life is charged with energies generated by the spirit of love within us, the words we speak have locked within them an intrinsic power to influence the lives of other people in some way or other.

However, our words must be received if they are to enter in and take root in the heart of another person. To the degree that the spirit of our love is selfless and mature, and to the degree that it is received by another, in that same measure do we touch and help to heal the hearts of others. Hence, the lives of those with whom we live and work can be changed for the better or they can be changed for the worse, depending upon the "holiness" or the "unholiness" of our love.

On the human level the ultimate in intimacy is reached when a husband and wife, in a highly spiritual experience of mutual self-surrender, give their total "yes" to each other in the marriage act. In their surrender of self to one another, the pro-creative energies of their love are released and new life comes forth in the existence of another human being. If the "yes" of mutual self-surrender on the human level is powerful enough to bring forth new life, then what must love on the divine level be like?

Oneness in the Trinity

From this it follows that human love seeks presence but intimacy requires union. However, oneness on the human level is not possible. No two human beings can ever be omnipresent to each other. Since love is God's essential energy, He seeks by His very nature to share His presence. But intimacy within the Trinity is satisfied with nothing less than oneness or omnipresence.

Within the mystery of the Godhead the insatiable longings in the heart of the Father to share His Being are generated eternally by the Spirit of His love. These longings move Him to make Himself present in another Person by communicating in fullness His own Holy Spirit of Love.

In the silent "yes" of His total and uninterrupted Self-Communication, the Father begets eternally His beloved Son. In the intimacy of the Spirit of Love, the Father is one with the Son. He is omnipresent to Him. That is why the Son shares fully in the divine nature of the Father.

The Son responds to the Father's complete

Self-Communication in the silent "yes" of His own total surrender of Self. He gives Himself back to the Father in the same Spirit of Love. In the omnipresence of Father and Son there is the divine intimacy of oneness because Father and Son share fully in the same Spirit of Love. Hence, the Son is the perfect Image of the Father. He is in full possession of all the energies of love which spring up eternally from the Father's heart. He possesses in fullness the infinite power and knowledge of the Father.

In the mystery of the Trinity, then, there is oneness in the divine essence, for the Father and the Son both share fully in the infinite power and knowledge generated by the Holy Spirit of Love. But they are distinct Persons because of the mutual Self-Communication in the uninterrupted flow of the Spirit of Love between Father and Son. It is the Holy Spirit, the third Person in the Trinity, Who brings about oneness in the Godhead and at the same time distinction in Persons.

Presence Beyond the Godhead

Since love is God's essential energy, He seeks to communicate His presence beyond the Godhead. He does this in the act of creating. The Eastern Fathers saw all of the uncreated energies of God's love centered in the Logos, the energy-filled pre-existing Word of God. Therefore, before anything comes into existence in time and space, it is already in existence in the thought-life of God. For example, before our physical birth, we pre-existed eternally in the thought-life of God. When God speaks His creative Word, the power of His Spirit of Love brings into existence the eternal desires and thoughts in His Heart.

The dynamic utterance of God is the first recorded event in the Old Testament. When He spoke His Word and sent forth His Spirit, His eternal plan to share Himself beyond the Trinitarian community became reality:

> Now the earth was a formless void,
>   there was darkness over the deep,
>   and God's spirit hovered over the water.
> God said, "Let there be light,"
>   and there was light (Genesis 1:2-3).

In God's first creative utterance the light, power and beauty of His inner life of love flashed through the darkness of the chaotic abyss and dispelled forever the inky-black night of the "formless void." Through speaking His All-Powerful Word, the brilliant radiance of His own uncreated energy of light was released in the universe. The "light" of His own presence in the universe is the first and most sublime of all the elements. Thus, God Himself is present in the universe for His light is inseparable from His divine nature.

It is through His All-Powerful Word, then, that the energies of God's own inner life of love are released and take form in the multiple expressions of beauty and power in the universe. God Himself is present in all of His creatures through the many manifestations of the uncreated energies coming forth from the inner life of the Trinity.

Reflection

God alone existed. Then He chose to call into being that which did not exist. In the act of creating, God sent forth the uncreated energies of His love through His All-Powerful Word and brought the universe into existence. While God is unknowable and unapproachable in His essence, He does communicate Himself to us in the energies which flow out of His Spirit of Love. Thus, God is present in all created reality because His energies are inseparable from His Divine Being.

One of the Eastern Fathers of the Church used the sun to illustrate their teaching that God does not communicate His essence but He does communicate Himself to us through His uncreated energies of love. The sun, like God, is unapproachable and inaccessible. Yet, the energies of light and heat which are of the very substance of the sun are present and active in the world. Those energies, inseparable from the sun itself, are absorbed by the things of earth and they bring forth new life in multiple forms.

The Hebrew people found the invisible Creator in the visible world and were led to profound feelings of wonder and gratitude. The overwhelming presence of God found in all creation seemed to baffle the psalmist:

> *Where could I go to escape your spirit?*
> *Where could I flee from your presence?*
> *If I climb the heavens, you are there,*
> *there too, if I lie in Sheol.*
> *If I flew to the point of sunrise,*
> *or westward across the sea,*
> *your hand would still be guiding me,*
> *your right hand holding me* (Psalm 139:7-10).

The psalmist was also keenly aware of the providence of God. He was very conscious of the activity of God in the universe as He sustains and directs it from moment to moment. He sings the praises of our provident God Who manifests His energetic love in the universe by the things He does:

> *. . . who covers the heavens with clouds,*
> *to provide the earth with rain,*

to produce fresh grass on the hillsides
and the plants that are needed by man,
who gives their food to the cattle
and to the young ravens when they cry
(Psalm 147:8-9).

In the Old Testament, however, God is seen not only as the Creator Who is present "at the point of sunrise" and "westward across the sea," but also as the Divine Lover Who sought to draw His people into the intimacy of His love. The Israelites gradually became aware of God's love for them as they experienced His saving acts in their behalf. The psalmist recalled some of the wonderful deeds Yahweh performed for his ancestors as they journeyed toward the Promised Land:

They demanded food, he sent them quails,
he satisfied them with the bread of heaven;
he opened the rock, the waters gushed
to flow through the desert like a river (Psalm
105:40-41).

Love is God's essential energy. When He extends His love beyond Himself, this "energy" is manifested in multiple ways. The beauty and power of all the known and unknown energies in every human being, in every living creature, in every particle of matter are but an extension of God's own essential energy of love. He is present in the beauty and warmth of light, in the power of wind, in the force of water and in countless other ways. Thus, God does not hide Himself in His unknowable essence, but He presents Himself to us in manifold ways through the power of His Spirit of Love when He speaks His All-Powerful Word.

3

Longing For Presence

Many people know the story of Saint Augustine. He struggled for years before he learned that God had made him for Himself. A radical change took place in his restless heart only when he came to realize through honest self-confrontation, that beneath his self-serving desires for the "good things of life" there was an unconscious longing for God.

Centuries before Augustine made his appearance on the human scene, Yahweh had been at work teaching the Israelites how to seek Him and how to find Him. The Book of Psalms, one of the most exquisite of all the books of the Old Testament, is a collection of the prayers of some of the Israelites who were seeking God with all their hearts. There is no doubt that these ancient writers drew very close to God and may be listed among the world's greatest mystics. While there were many writers of the psalms, for our purpose we will use the singular, the psalmist.

Conditions For True Spirituality

In Psalm 24 the psalmist set down the conditions for all genuine spirituality. He posed a question and then he himself answered it:

> *Who has the right to climb the mountain of*
> *Yahweh,*
> *who the right to stand in his holy place?*
> *He whose hands are clean,*
> *whose heart is pure,*
> *whose soul does not pay homage to worth-*
> *less things*
> *and who never swears to a lie* (Psalm 24:3-4).

These words of the psalmist reveal that God, the All-Holy One, allows us to draw near to Him. But what are the conditions? How can we, mere creatures, draw near to a God Who is unapproachable and inaccessible because of His transcendent holiness? The psalmist who was longing for a close relationship to God learned the answer.

While reflecting prayerfully on his life, he was given the insight that he could not draw near to God until he acknowledged and abandoned his self-indulgent desires and his pretentious ways. This insight found expression in his prayer. In the future he would have to "purify" his heart from all attachment to anything that would draw him away from God and he would have to be honest in all of his social relationships.

Before Conversion

Up to this time the psalmist gloried in his own power and excellence. With great zest he sought to fulfill the illusory and self-serving desires and thoughts that filled his heart. In his forgetfulness of the God to Whom he owed his existence, he "turned his back on wisdom." Relying on his human powers alone, he was unable to discern what was true and what was false in the events and situations of his immediate world. It did not occur to him to question the words coming from the false prophets who were leading the people away from their covenant relationship with God. Nor was he aware of his inclination to believe the deceptions hidden in the popular opinions so widespread in his day. Consequently, the psalmist was deceived and that which he said and did wrought "mischief and deceit" in the lives of others.

Warped by his self-seeking ways and the false security of his own self-sufficiency, the psalmist could not "detect and detest his guilt" because he saw himself with "too flattering an eye." However, deep down in his heart he was frustrated. He longed to become more intimate with God, but for some reason, unknown to himself, he could not get close to Him. Others drew near to God. Why couldn't he?

Unable to restrain His affection for this self-sufficient person, God's holy love gradually began to penetrate the hardened heart of the psalmist. The efforts of this psalmist to impress others with his importance and his cleverness no longer brought him the self-exaltation that he had formerly enjoyed. Instead, he became deeply troubled as he began to experience feelings of inauthenticity, anxiety and loneliness.

As the irresistible beam of divine love penetrated the heart of the psalmist, he began to recognize in himself the tendencies to be arrogant, resentful, self-righteous and even somewhat deceitful in order to make his point or get his way. His efforts to check these inclinations through sheer will-power alone proved to be futile. Frightened by an intolerable helplessness, the psalmist finally turned to God and cried out to Him in great anguish:

> To you, Yahweh, I lift up my soul,
> O my God (Psalm 25:1-2).

Conversion of Heart

The process of conversion had begun in the heart of the psalmist when he became aware of his brokenness and acknowledged before God all of the miseries of his heart. As he stood before the riches of his all-loving God, he was no longer the self-righteous and self-reliant person he had been. With a new awareness of God he now addressed Him in a spirit of true humility:

From the depths I call to you, Yahweh,
Lord, listen to my cry for help!
Listen compassionately to my pleading!
(Psalm 130:1-2).

The psalmist's humility before God was nothing more than seeing clearly what his position was in relation to Him. It was now a position of helplessness and dependence. His attitude became that of a free person who had come to realize that his freedom was complete when he recognized and admitted his sinfulness and turned to God in total dependence on Him. Gone were the days of habitual servitude to his whims and compulsions!

As the psalmist became more conscious of God's love for him he was no longer afraid to face himself honestly. With all defenses down, he now approached God with complete confidence and trust in His love:

> Yet, *since you love sincerity of heart,*
> *teach me the secrets of wisdom* (Psalm 51:6).

In this prayer the psalmist was praying for the wisdom to know the hidden faults he had not yet discovered in himself. As he entered into new levels of consciousness, he began to see that many of his personal problems were rooted in those movements of his heart that he could not subdue through sheer will-power. He began to put the blame for many of his problems where it properly belonged — on himself. With full confidence in God's unwavering love for him he asked to be forgiven:

> *If you never overlooked our sins, Yahweh,*
> *Lord, could anyone survive?*
> > *But you do forgive us:*
> > *and for that we revere you* (Psalm 130:3-4).

Now, fully aware of his total inability to mend his own brokenness, the repentant psalmist surrendered his whole being to God:

> *My sacrifice is this broken spirit,*
> > *you will not scorn*
> > *this crushed and broken heart* (Psalm 51:17).

These words came from the heart of one who at last fully understood the weakness of the human condition. Through suffering and humiliation his craving to control his own life independently of God was finally shattered. His conscious and unconscious efforts to rationalize his way out of his obligations ceased when he offered his "broken spirit" to Yahweh. When he uttered this prayer, the psalmist was fully confident that he would not be rejected. Far from rejecting the repentant psalmist, God drew him more deeply into the mystery of His love.

As the psalmist became more aware of his nearness to God he moved into new levels of self-perception, self-understanding and self-acceptance. The healing warmth of divine love which he now experienced made him conscious of an entirely new relationship between God and himself. His anxieties diminished and he began to feel the inner peace of the divine presence, an entirely new experience for him. He now prayed:

> Yahweh is near to the broken-hearted,
> he helps those whose spirit is crushed (Psalm 34:18).

Though sin had entered his life, it was the means by which the psalmist became conscious of the irresistible power of God's holy love. This love penetrated his whole being: body, soul and spirit. In the experience of being healed by God's love he began to see the need to develop mature and loving relationships to all other people. Confident that the God of Love would now "re-create" him anew, the psalmist prayed yet more ardently for a change of his inner values and attitudes:

God, *create a clean heart in me,*
put into me a new and constant spirit . . .
(Psalm 51:10).

In beautiful imagery the psalmist described the true inner peace that he began to enjoy because of his humble attitude toward God and his complete confidence in Him. He could now speak of peace to others because there was no longer any malice in his own heart. He had simply stifled his disturbed spirit by holding fast to the Lord, just as a child quiets its fears by clinging to its mother:

Yahweh, my heart has no lofty ambitions,
my eyes do not look too high.
I am not concerned with great affairs
or marvels beyond my scope.
Enough for me to keep my soul tranquil and
quiet
like a child in its mother's arms,
as content as a child that has been weaned
(Psalm 131:1-2)

As the psalmist became more conscious of the divine presence operating in his life, it began to dawn on him that God was drawing him into an intense and intimate relationship with Himself. There were moments when he was very much aware of God's tender love for him personally. He speaks of his intimacy with God in these words:

> The close secret of Yahweh
>   belongs to them who fear him,
>   his covenant also,
>   to bring them knowledge (Psalm 25:14).

Reflection

One may well assume that the psalmist was not a notoriously evil man even before his conversion. He really wanted to draw nearer to God, but he was unable to do so because he was caught and held in the web of spiritual mediocrity. Quick to note the faults of others, he saw very little in himself that he considered to be reprehensible. It was only through suffering and struggle that he finally acknowledged his own brokenness and then abandoned himself to God in an experience of utter helplessness.

As the psalmist opened himself ever more completely to the healing power of divine love, he began to notice in his own character those very traits which he had found to be so blameworthy in others: namely, his self-centered and pretentious ways. As his relationship to God became more intense and absorbing, his quickness to find fault in others and his tendency to rationalize away his own failures and shortcomings lessened.

The more the psalmist allowed God to enter into the circumstances of his daily life situations, the more did he move into that inner wholeness and integration he so ardently desired. His fears vanished and he experienced more than ever before God's personal love for him penetrating and transforming his whole being:

I need only say, "I am slipping,"
and your love, Yahweh,
immediately supports me;
and in the middle of all my troubles
you console me and make me happy
(Psalm 94:18-19).

4

The Promise of a New Heart

As the history of Israel unfolded, the prophets played a significant role in the spiritual development of the people. Indeed, some of the later prophets began to speak more specifically about a time when God Himself would enter more directly into their lives. Jeremiah, in particular, paved the way for the New Covenant of the Christian Era by showing how intimate each person's contact with God should be. Ezekiel's teachings helped to prepare for the New Testament doctrine of salvation through grace.

Circumcision of Heart

Over the centuries the prophets, psalmists and other devout people lived according to the Law of God as they "walked humbly" with Him.

The prophet Jeremiah, however, could see that the external imposition of the Law was not bringing about the desired conversion of the Israelite people as a whole.

Jeremiah lived before and during the tragic years of the Babylonian Captivity. Because of his gentle and affectionate nature, he suffered great inner anguish as he carried out his mission of warning the people to lead better lives lest they be destroyed. His intense suffering purified his heart and gradually brought him to great intimacy with God. It was through the experience of his own radical conversion of heart that this prophet began to call for a radical inner renewal in the hearts of the Israelite people.

In his teachings Jeremiah proceeded to prepare the Israelites for a new development in their covenant relationship with God by talking about "circumcision of heart." The rite of circumcision had been given to their father Abraham centuries before as a sign of their covenant relationship with God:

> *Now this is my Covenant*
> > *which you are to maintain between myself*
> > > *and you,*
> > *and your descendants after you:*
> > *all your males must be circumcised*
> > > > > > (Genesis 17:10)

While circumcision was the exterior sign of their covenant relationship with God, Jeremiah preached that it was meaningless unless it was accompanied by "circumcision of the heart." Since intimacy with God demands a heart that is "purified," the heart must be "circumcised" of all falsehood and slavish attachments:

> *Circumcise yourselves for Yahweh;*
> *off with the foreskin of your hearts . . .*
>
> (Jeremiah 4:4).

This circumcision of the heart would necessitate the personal decision to live at an entirely new level of consciousness. It would mean adopting a brand new attitude toward God in an abandonment of all prejudice, false values and bad habits. This new relationship with God would mean living a life-style pleasing to Him in every aspect of one's human endeavors and encounters.

Law in the Heart

In connection with circumcision of heart, Jeremiah preached about the dawn of a New Covenant in which God would write the Law, not on tablets of stone, but on the human heart:

> *Deep within them I will plant my Law,*
> *writing it on their hearts.*

> *Then I will be their God*
> *and they shall be my people*
> (Jeremiah 31:33).

In this Covenant relationship no new obligations would be imposed, but people would observe the Law from inner desire and conviction. In this way Jeremiah gave primacy to the interior value of obedience to God out of love for Him. He told the people that God would "forgive their inquity and never call their sin to mind" if they would "Learn to Know Yahweh!" (Jeremiah 31:34). Biblically, "knowledge of God" means more than having mere intellectual knowledge about Him. It means entering into an intimate relationship with Him through "circumcision of heart" and returning "love for love" at ever deepening levels.

A New Heart and a New Spirit

Ezekiel, like Jeremiah, lived during the days of the Babylonian Captivity. He also helped to prepare the people for the inauguration of a New Covenant between God and themselves. He talked about a "new heart" and a "new spirit" which would be given them. Ezekiel taught that the New Covenant would not come about as a result of human effort because God alone could bring about a "new creation" in His people. He

Himself would provide for the cleansing of their hearts of "defilement" and "idols":

> I shall pour clean water over you
>   and you will be cleansed;
> I shall cleanse you of all your defilement
>   and all your idols.
> I shall give you a new heart,
>   and put a new spirit in you;
> I shall remove the heart of stone from your bodies
>   and give you a heart of flesh instead.
> I shall put my spirit in you,
>   and make you keep my laws
>   and sincerely respect my observances
>   (Ezekiel 36:25-27).

Ezekiel was speaking of some future time when God would remove the "heart of stone" (a closed mind) and replace it with a "heart of flesh." The Spirit of God Who creates and gives life would become the principle of an inner renewal which would make the observance of God's Law possible. Hence, it would be under the impulse of God's own Spirit of Love that people would finally fulfill the requirements of the Law. Like life-giving water the Spirit of God would bring forth wholeness and integrity in the human personality. Thus it would be through the activity of the Holy Spirit of God's love that human hearts would be transformed and "re-created."

The prophet Joel added a new note to the teachings of Ezekiel by proclaiming that the Spirit of God would not be given to the Israelites only but to all people of all nations:

After this I will pour out my spirit
on all mankind (Joel 3:1).

Reflection

The fulfillment of the prophecy of Joel some four hundred years later proves to be the most significant event in human history. The New Covenant relationship with God which had been foretold by the prophets of old began to unfold at that precise moment when Jesus, now the Risen Lord, poured the Spirit of His love into the hearts of His disciples in the Upper Room on Pentecost Sunday. This prophecy continues to be fulfilled in the life of every one of us who receives Christian Baptism, for it is in this sacrament that the same Spirit of Love is poured into the heart of the baptized person.

However, baptism is only the beginning of our journey to intimacy with God. We can go through life unaware of this Indwelling, unless we take time regularly for silence, meditation and humble reflection. In this way we develop "listening hearts," grow in true discernment and begin to distinguish between the ego-promptings of our hearts and the insights given by the Holy Spirit of Love. To the degree that we become conscious of the activity of the Holy Spirit dwelling within us, to that degree will our human love be transformed and made holy.

Love is God's essential energy and holiness is the very essence of His inner life of love. Unlike human love God's love does not have that element of selfishness which renders our love vindictive and "unholy" when it is unaccepted or disappointed. Human nature had taken on unholy tendencies when Adam and Eve rejected God's love. They deliberately broke off communication with Him by refusing to listen to His Word.

However, God never "gives up" on us, His most precious creatures, because His Spirit of Love is always holy. It is His consuming desire for us that moves Him to continue to love us in spite of our repeated failures. It is through the activity of His Spirit within us that "hearts of stone" are turned into "hearts of flesh" and unholy love becomes holy. Saint Paul tells us what human love, transformed by the Spirit of God's holy love, is like:

Love is always patient and kind;
  it is never jealous;
  love is never boastful or conceited;
  it is never rude or selfish;
  it does not take offence, and is not resentful.
Love takes no pleasure in other people's sins
  but delights in the truth;
  it is always ready to excuse, to trust, to
  hope, and to endure whatever comes
                              (I Corinthians 13:4-7).

5

Presence Through the Word

As the history of the Israelite people unfolded, the dynamic energies of God's Spirit of Love were released again and again through His Word. Each time that God spoke, the power of His Spirit became operative and active in the hearts of those people who were open to receive His divine communication. God was present to His People in the inspired Word of Scripture, in the "Ten Words" He spoke to Moses on Mt. Sinai, in His words of admonition and loving concern, in His call to the prophets and in countless other ways.

Hebraic Meaning of Word

In order to grasp more fully the Scriptural approach to grace, it will be helpful to have some understanding of the rich biblical meaning of "word." In the Hebrew language, "word" has reference not only to the intellectual concept it conveys, but also to the potential locked within it to effect what it signifies. Biblically, the word of God is dynamic. This means that it is endowed with power. When God speaks, His Word achieves something. It is creative and life-giving because there is locked within it a power which brings into reality the meaning behind the Word.

For both sacred writers and eastern theologians, the Word of Scripture is more than the "bearer" of information about God. For them, the Word is the transmitter of the power and energies of God's Holy Spirit of Love into the universe and the hearts of human beings.

Presence Through the Word of Scripture

Who can know the thoughts of God unless He Himself communicates them to us? Since the words of Scripture contain the revealed thoughts of God, they provide us with information about the nature of God, His relationship to the human race and to all created reality. However, the inspired Word in the Bible can do more than merely impart information. For the person who ponders Scripture with a "listening heart," the Word can be the bearer of divine energies of love which flow out of the heart of God into the heart of the receiver of the Word. Actually, the Word of Scripture is the medium through which the dynamic power of the "thought-life" of God is transmitted and brought into the "thought-life" of the receiver. In this way human thoughts become divinized and human hearts become changed.

Hence, the Word of God communicates to us the divine energies of God Himself. The Word comes from God and it cannot fail; it had its way in the unfolding of the history of Israel; it will go on having its way as long as human history continues to unfold:

> Yes, as the rain and the snow come down from the heavens and do not return without watering the earth, making it yield and giving growth to provide seed for the sower and bread for the eating, so the word that goes from my mouth does not return to me empty, without carrying out my will and succeeding in what it was sent to do (Isaiah 55:10-11).

Presence Through the Law

God manifested His presence to the Israelites by pouring forth the energies of His love in manifold ways. He satisfied His longings to be with them by accompanying them as they journeyed through the desert. He "spoke" to them through theophanies and various other visible signs. Yahweh was present in the cloud that guided them by day and in the fire that led them by night. He was present in the manna and quails that fed them and in the life-giving water that quenched their thirst. He manifested His uncreated energies of power and glory in the theophany at Sinai and arranged to be present with His people in the Tent of Meeting. However, in order to bring the "thoughts" of His people into communion with His own "thoughts," God communicated Himself to the Israelites in a still more direct way. This was through the Law.

Throughout the history of Israel the Law in which the Covenant relationship was rooted was the verbal expression of God's will for His people. Hence, the Decalogue and the various codes of the Covenant were not just collections of impersonal legislation, but they were the dynamic utterance of God expressed in human language. It was Yahweh's intent to impart Wisdom to His people by putting them in direct contact with His own thoughts regarding their relationship to Him and one another.

Some of the writers of Wisdom Literature saw that the Law was the same creative Word by which the universe was made when "God's spirit hovered over the water." They believed it was to be obeyed not as a duty, but because the Law was truth coming from God Himself. They pointed out that it meant basically guidance or instruction. However, it was obedience to the Law which produced wisdom, joy, peace and liberty in the hearts of those who obeyed it. It was their loving docility to God that effected transformation in the hearts of those whose lives were governed by it.

Psalm 119 is a reflection in praise of the Law. In this beautiful prayer the psalmist shows that true obedience to the Law cannot be mechanical or legalistic. He shows the excellence of a loving attitude toward it. The psalmist delights in the Law because it is the Word of God and obedience to it puts him in close communion with God. Since the Law is an expression of God's will for the Israelites, the psalmist conceives it as being perfect:

> *I have noticed limitations to all perfection, but your commandment has no limits at all* (Psalm 119:96).

Presence Through Words of Concern

It was through the prophet Isaiah that Yahweh lamented the social failure of His cherished people when they reached the limit of their depravity, no longer making a distinction between moral good and evil. Through Isaiah, Yahweh let the Israelites know His great displeasure and concern regarding their corruption:

> *Woe to those who call evil good, and good evil,*
> *who substitute darkness for light*
> *and light for darkness,*
> *who substitute bitter for sweet*
> *and sweet for bitter (Isaiah 5:20).*

Yet, the divine wrath should not be seen in terms of human peevishness and revenge. Because His love is holy, God never takes revenge. He can always be depended upon as One Who will not come to destroy:

> *I am the Holy One in your midst*
> *and have no wish to destroy (Hosea 11:9).*

However, the mystery of God's love did not prevent the inevitable disaster which befell the Israelites when the Assryrians invaded their land. They brought upon themselves their own chastisement. Whether the Chosen People were suffering at the hands of other nations or whether they were suffering the pangs of repentance because of their sinful ways, the mystery of God's loving presence through His Word never failed.

The long years in Babylon had given the people a sense of being forgotten and forsaken by Yahweh. Actually, this is not the way it was. Isaiah's portrayal of God's never-changing affection is one of the most touching expressions of divine love in the whole Bible. Like a father caressing his frightened child, God whispered words of endearment to His exiled people, driving out fear and mistrust:

> For I, Yahweh, your God,
>   I am holding you by the right hand;
>   I tell you, "Do not be afraid,
>   I will help you" (Isaiah 41:13).

Presence in the Prophetic Call

In reading the Old Testament we learn how the prophets were called by God to be the human bearers of His dynamic Word. The Word of God came to them as an irresistible force. In the acceptance of the Call, the personality of the prophet was invaded by the personality of Yahweh. Having heard the Word in his own heart, the prophet was now ready to transmit it to others. When the prophets spoke, they communicated to the people the thoughts of God. It was His uncreated energies which brought into reality the thought behind their words.

In powerful language the prophet Isaiah describes his own prophetic call which came to him in the temple. His experience of the awe-some holiness and majestic beauty of God was something that he would never forget.

While Isaiah was at prayer, God gave him a "glimpse" of Himself seated on a high throne sur-rounded by the heavenly court. The temple building shook with vibrations coming from the chant of the celestial choir proclaiming the holi-ness of God:

Holy, holy, holy is Yahweh Sabaoth.
His glory fills the whole earth (Isaiah 6:3).

Isaiah was completely shattered when he found himself in the holy presence of God. He suddenly became conscious of the unholiness in his own life and the lives of the Israelite people. The over-whelming contrast between God's holiness and human pettiness and self-centeredness made Isaiah shrink back in shame. As the majesty, glory and holiness of God's love penetrated his consciousness, he gained a new awareness of human sinfulness:

What a wretched state I am in!
I am lost, for I am a man of unclean lips
and I live among a people of unclean lips,
and my eyes have looked at the King,
    Yahweh Sabaoth (Isaiah 6:5).

In delightful imagery the prophet then tells how the seraph cleansed him of the sinfulness in his heart and communicated divine holiness to him:

> Then one of the seraphs flew to me,
>   holding in his hand a live coal
>   which he had taken from the altar
>   with a pair of tongs.
> With this he touched my mouth and said:
>   "See now, this has touched your lips,
>   your sin is taken away,
>   your iniquity is purged" (Isaiah 6:6-7).

Holiness in human beings comes only through sharing in the holiness of God. The self-centered and unholy love in the heart of Isaiah was destroyed by the fire of the live coal which the seraph took from the altar. Transformed by the fire of divine love, Isaiah could now discern the wishes of God in his regard:

> Then I heard the voice of the Lord saying:
> "Whom shall I send?
>   Who will be our messenger?" (Isaiah 6:8).

Isaiah responded without hesitation:

> Here I am, send me (Isaiah 6:8).

Isaiah's awesome encounter with God had a profound effect on him for the remainder of his life. Having become deeply conscious of his own brokenness, he could now detect the brokenness in the hearts of others. He could now pass on the Word to others only because he himself had received it into his own heart. At last Isaiah was ready to go to the sinful people of his nation who relied solely on human wisdom. Without fear he would confront these people with the Wisdom which flows out of the holy love-life of God.

The Word of God is not something abstract. It is not something to be submitted merely to the power of human reasoning. On the contrary, it involves a personal decision in the surrender of one's whole being to God. It was through the submission of their minds and wills to God that the prophets of old entered into mystical communion with Him and came into the possession of His own Word-Wisdom.

This was the experience of Isaiah in the temple. In the acknowledgement of his own brokenness and in the total surrender of himself to God, he made himself ready to receive the Word of God. Having received the Word into his own heart, he was empowered to transmit this Word to others.

Reflection

God has placed contemplative powers within the heart of every human being. Yet, why is it that there are so few contemplative and prophetic people in our world today? Why are there not more Mother Teresas in religious communities and more Dag Hammarskjolds in the political arena?

All genuine prayer is potentially contemplative and is within the reach of anyone who does not hold back in responding to God's personal invitation to love. In contemplative prayer we come to know the great love of God which empowers us to surrender to Him ever more totally. However, this prayer is like a seed: the soil must be suitable and the conditions for growth must be favorable.

If our prayer is to take on a contemplative dimension, more is needed than merely being faithful to our obligations of prayer. More is required than merely getting satisfaction out of prayer. Contemplative prayer takes place in the heart and not on the lips or in the mind. We all know the experience of longing for the presence of an absent loved one. In contemplative prayer, the lips and the mind are quiet while the heart longs for the presence of God. Contemplative prayer, therefore, is a deep level of prayer which leads one beyond words and thoughts to an awareness of the presence of the Trinity within, loving us intimately from moment to moment.

We might ask then, "How does one move into contemplative prayer?" First of all, if we desire to move into deep levels of prayer, we must take sufficient time for prayer each day. We must be convinced that our relationship to God has top priority in our lives since growth in holiness is based on this relationship and on nothing else. Christian holiness is more than the practice of the social graces, human courtesies and the exercise of "good common sense." It cannot be reduced to mere ethical behavior or good moral conduct through the exercise of human willpower alone.

To be contemplative, prayer must lead to new and deeper insights about oneself, one's relationship to God and to other people. Discovering the contemplative dimension of prayer is a new self-discovery on an entirely different level than that of the psychological. This prayer moves one into profound depths of faith-living and into the realm of genuine spiritual values.

In order to discover the Word of the Father present in the Spirit of Love within us, we need regular periods of silence and solitude in our lives. Over-absorption in endless activities makes contemplative prayer impossible. We so readily find time to do those things that we like to do, those things which bring us pleasure. But without the discipline of taking time consistently to be alone with God in silent prayer, the contemplative powers within us do not develop.

As we deepen in interior prayer, we become more aware of our littleness before God and come to an awareness of our absolute dependence on Him. A recognition of our personal need for God, and an acknowledgement of our sinful tendencies and complete abandonment of self to His love and mercy must precede the experience of discovering God within. In other words, the interior dispositions of humility, contrition and trusting surrender of self are indispensable for the inner peace and quiet joy that accompany greater familiarity with God.

However, the interior dispositions of humility, contrition and trust must be guarded and nourished constantly lest they give way to attitudes of self-complacency and self-sufficiency. Meditating on the Scripture daily and learning about the interior life through study and the proper spiritual reading are powerful means for helping us to be aware of our constant need for God.

It is contemplative prayer, the discovery of God dwelling within us, which makes us powerful and effective instruments in continuing the redemptive work of Jesus Christ. In sharing the fruits of our contemplation with others, we become effective at the spiritual level in the lives of others regardless of what our apostolate may be.

To the degree that we allow God to take over in our lives through our surrender of self to Him, to that degree do we become one with Him in mind and heart. As we abandon ourselves to His personal love for us, He transforms our human powers to know and love with divine Wisdom and divine Love. Empowered with divine Wisdom, we meet the physical, mental and spiritual needs of others with the attitude and values of Christ Himself. Enriched with divine Love, we go forth daily to assist Christ in His sacred work of reconciling people with God and with one another.

6

The Beginning of Wisdom

The desire for wisdom is a yearning that is present in the heart of every human being. This longing is put there by God Himself and is nothing less than an insatiable desire for Him Who is Eternal Wisdom. That is why every human being, either consciously or unconsciously, longs for God. That also is the reason why every human heart is "restless" until it is ready to receive the "Wisdom" that God wishes to impart.

Wisdom Literature

Centuries ago collections of writings known as "Wisdom Literature" flourished in many cultures of the ancient East in various literary forms. Much of this literature was in the form of proverbs, riddles, parables and poetry. These wisdom writings dealt with the meaning of life. The "wisemen" or sages drew from their own personal experiences in their everyday living and offered suggestions for coping with human problems.

The earliest Wisdom Literature of the Israelites resembled that of their neighboring countries. Their collections of maxims and proverbs for obtaining wisdom became a guide for others.

The later Israelite writers, however, developed their own concept of wisdom and taught that human wisdom alone is incapable of grasping the full meaning of life. They learned from personal experience and prayerful reflection that such wisdom does not provide the perception needed to get to the root of human problems. They drew the conclusion, therefore, that human wisdom in itself is incapable of coping with the deeper realities of one's daily life situations.

The wisdom writers gradually began to notice that their general well-being was related to their own inner attitude toward God. As they observed self, neighbor and the created realities around them, they discovered God in the setting of their everyday situations. They began to see that the practical details of their human endeavors and encounters were the "raw material" of their own relationship to God.

As these sages searched ever more earnestly for the true meaning of life and became more acutely aware of the limits of finite wisdom, their hearts became more attuned to the insights that God was sharing with them. Their intimacy with Him deepened as they gradually learned that true wisdom comes from a Source much more reliable than mere human reasoning. Eventually, the conviction that Wisdom is rooted in God and is communicated to the "humble of heart" became a significant theological development in Israel's wisdom literature:

> All wisdom is from the Lord,
> and it is his own for ever (Ecclesiasticus 1:1).

> To fear the Lord
> is the beginning of wisdom . . . (Ecclesiasticus 1:14).

The basic doctrine that "fear of the Lord" is essential for true wisdom has captured the attention of contemporary Scripture scholars. "Fear of the Lord" in Israelite wisdom literature carries no connotations of fright or dread before God because of His almighty power. On the other hand, it connotes a "listening heart," a heart that is open and eager to receive the "Wisdom" that God wishes to impart. It connotes reverence for Him, a spirit of dependence on Him and obedience to Him out of love.

Wisdom and Daily Living

Ben Sira, the author of the Book of Ecclesiasticus, was one of these wise and experienced observers of life. His contribution to Wisdom Literature is especially rich in its teachings that true wisdom flows from a deep personal relationship with God. This writer shows that a "listening heart" is the very foundation for wholesome and healthy relationships to God, self, others and all created reality.

In Chapter One of Ecclesiasticus the author deals with the mystery of Wisdom. He affirms that all wisdom has its source in God and that He imparts His Wisdom to all who love and revere Him:

> *One only is wise, terrible indeed,*
> *seated on his throne, the Lord,*
> *He himself has created her (Wisdom),*
> *looked on her and assessed her,*
> *and poured her out on all his works*
> *to be with all mankind as his gift,*
> *and he conveyed her to those who love him*
> (Ecclesiasticus 1:8-10).

In delightful imagery Ben Sira speaks of the total well-being that is enjoyed by those who have listening hearts. Fear of the Lord clears the way for the entrance of Wisdom. When Wisdom comes, it brings wholeness to the total person: body, soul and spirit:

> *The fear of the Lord will gladden the heart*
> *giving happiness and joy and long life.*

> *To fear the Lord is the perfection of wisdom;*
> *she intoxicates them with her fruits;*
> *she fills their whole house with their heart's*
> *desire,*
> *and their storerooms with her produce.*
> *The fear of the Lord is the crown of wisdom;*
> *it makes peace and health to flourish*
> (Ecclesiasticus 1:12; 16-18).

The writer then notes some of the inner dispositions of heart necessary for the acquisition of true wisdom. He extols the patient man who "holds out till the time comes" for "his joy will break out in the end." Others will recognize his prudence and listen to what he says. On the other hand, the unrestrained man who speaks under compulsion will eventually spoil things for himself.

Ben Sira continues to speak of wisdom as the reward of faithful obedience. He teaches that obedience, tempered with humility and gentleness, is pleasing to the Lord because it carries one beyond legalism and mere conformity. He maintains that this kind of obedience assures authenticity.

This author condemns the use of pretentious words for the purpose of making a "good" impression on others. He warns that arrogance, self-exaltation, boastfulness and a deceitful heart will eventually bring embarrassment.

Wisdom and Suffering

In Chapter Two Ben Sira speaks of the suffering that comes to those who seek God with all their hearts. He knows from personal experience that serving God is not without its trials. The sage teaches that one should remain calm and unafraid when suffering does come. He urges reliance on God and a "clinging" to Him as the means of emerging victoriously. A heart that is open to God's wishes gives one access to God's great mercy.

Ben Sira points out that misfortune and humiliations are allowed by God because they purify the heart. If a man continues to trust, God will come to his defense; if he is sincere, he has reason to hope; if he is devoted and obedient, he can anticipate God's mercy. Even if a man sins, God forgives and comes to the rescue of "the contrite of heart" because He is compassionate and merciful.

At the end of the chapter, Ben Sira admonishes those who compromise their religion in time of misfortune and affliction. He warns others not to be led astray by the "wisdom" which relies too heavily on human reasoning. This wisdom is, indeed, incapable of grasping the full meaning of life. Such "wisdom" often suggests illusory solutions which increase rather than diminish human problems. The sage invites all "to fall into the hands of the Lord" through reverence for God and devoted obedience to Him. Such attitudes must be present in the heart for the beginning of wisdom.

Reflection

The human heart was made to receive the "Wisdom" of God. But the silencing of our hearts to receive this Wisdom tends to be largely an unknown art in our contemporary society. Rather, the inherent longings of the human heart for communion with God are ignored and repressed in the rapid and hectic pace of a society preoccupied with the burdens, cares and pleasures of today's world. Few people seem to be aware of the need to take time daily just to "relax" with the Lord.

As ruler of the Israelite people, King Solomon gradually came to recognize his need for the kind of Wisdom which comes from God alone. Pondering his progress in prayer could be helpful to us.

As successor on David's throne, Solomon began to recognize his own personal inadequacies. He observed that his human judgments were not improving conditions in his kingdom but rather were creating new problems. The conscientious ruler then recognized the need to discern between the true good and the apparent good (evil in disguise) in dealing with the practical affairs in the government of his people. It gradually dawned on him that he needed help from God. Busy administrator though he was, Solomon began to take time regularly from his heavy schedule to pray for a "listening heart" that he might grow in discernment and discretion under Divine Wisdom:

> Give your servant a heart to understand
> how to discern between good and evil,
> for who could govern this people of yours
> that is so great? (1 Kings 3:9).

We may well assume that Solomon did not present his request to the Lord on one occasion only, but that he repeated his prayer frequently. The author of the Book of Wisdom shows how Solomon's prayer deepened and became more intense:

> *I turned to the Lord and entreated him,*
> *with all my heart I said:*
> *"God of our ancestors, Lord of mercy, . . .*
> *grant me Wisdom, consort of your throne*
> *and do not reject me*
> *from the number of your children"*
>   (Wisdom 8:21; 9:1-4).

As Solomon's heart opened still more to receive the Wisdom that God was imparting to him, he became keenly aware of his own shortcomings. He discovered in himself the tendency to listen to the "ego-promptings" of his own heart in the decisions that he was making. Consequently, his prayer became humble as he acknowledged his human weakness and his failure to comprehend the ways of God:

> *For I am your servant, son of your serving*
> *maid, a feeble man, with little time to live,*
> *with small understanding of justice and the laws*
>   (Wisdom 9:5).

"Fear of the Lord" was now a new attitude in Solomon's heart. The more he opened his heart in prayer to listen to the divine thoughts God was communicating to him, the more did he become conscious of God's immense love for him. To make those decisions which would be most pleasing to God became his greatest concern. So he prayed:

Despatch her (Wisdom) from the holy heavens,
send her forth from your throne of glory
*   to help and to toil with me*
*   and teach me what is pleasing to you,*
since she knows and understands everything
                                    (Wisdom 9:10).

The sacred writer then reinforces his earlier teaching that no one can know the thoughts of God unless He Himself communicates them to us. To whom does He communicate His secrets? He shares them with the humble of heart; to those who grow in "fear of the Lord"; to those who develop "listening hearts" through faithful prayer. Indeed, these are the people who help to shape the course of human history according to God's loving plan for the human race, because the decisions they make in their daily life situations are most pleasing to Him:

As for your intention,
*   who could have learnt it,*
*   had you not granted Wisdom*
*   and sent your holy spirit from above?*
Thus have the paths of those on earth
*   been straightened*
*   and men been taught what pleases you,*
*   and saved, by Wisdom* (Wisdom 9:17-18).

7

Communication of
Divine Wisdom

The inspired authors of Sacred Scripture
were people chosen by God to put His divine
thoughts into human language. Every sentence
in their writings has bearing in some way or
other on the fundamental relationship between
the divine and the human.

Under the God-revealing beam of divine
light, the writers of Wisdom Literature, in particular, were given extraordinary insights into
the nature of God and they became the world's
most eminent theologians. Under the self-reveal-
ing beam of divine love, these same writers per-
ceived human nature with unexcelled clarity and
became the world's most distinguished depth-
psychologists.

In the later wisdom writings the eternal pre-
existing Word of God, sometimes identified as

the *Logos*, is personified as the *Wisdom of God*. Several of the writers presented Wisdom as a woman who spoke about her characteristics and her function in the universe. In these writings the authors began to attribute to Wisdom those operations which are characteristic of the Word and the Spirit.

The Inner Life of God

In Chapter Seven of the Book of Wisdom the sage sings the praises of Wisdom. In his treatment of her nature and dignity, he draws our attention to the beauty and excellence of God's uncreated energies of love.

The writer chooses his words with great care in his endeavor to show that Wisdom possesses characteristics that are uniquely divine. In a series of highly descriptive words the author delineates the sublimity and the power of the Wisdom of God.

Locked within the Wisdom of God are all the uncreated energies generated eternally by the Holy Spirit of His love:

> *For within her is a spirit*
>   *intelligent, holy,*
>   *unique, manifold, subtle,*
>   *active, incisive, unsullied,*
>   *lucid, invulnerable, benevolent, sharp,*

> *irresistible, beneficent, loving to man,*
> *steadfast, dependable, unperturbed, . . .*
> (Wisdom 7:22-23).

It is through the Spirit of God's holy love that His Wisdom is intelligent. Wisdom is so intelligent that she knows all that there is to know. Therefore, God's thoughts are sound because His reasoning is unerring.

The Wisdom of God is holy because she is begotten by His Holy Spirit of Love. The sacred writer proclaims that Wisdom is flawless and faultless. There is no trace of hypocrisy or partiality in God's holy thought-life. Since Wisdom is all-holy, she transcends all that is created.

Because the Spirit of God is unique, the Wisdom of God is unique. There is no other wisdom comparable to her. In the Godhead there is oneness; yet, when God pours forth His Wisdom into the universe, she becomes diverse in her activity.

The sacred writer points out that the Wisdom of God, His divine thought-life, is subtle. By this he means that divine Wisdom eludes the grasp of human comprehension. Since she shares fully in the life-giving power generated by the Spirit of Love, Wisdom is capable of producing not mere existence but also movement and life. In this way the Wisdom of God is active in the universe.

There is nothing vague or ambiguous in the

activity of Wisdom because the Spirit in her is incisive, keen and acute. Whatever comes forth from God through the power of His Spirit in Wisdom is good and perfectly ordered in every way. In spite of her contact with the beings she pervades, Wisdom remains unsullied. Wisdom will always be unsullied and untarnished because the Spirit of God in her is all-holy.

The Spirit in Wisdom is lucid, invulnerable, benevolent, and sharp. Coming forth from God, Wisdom is suffused with His light and she radiates His light. She cannot be conquered by darkness because she is immune to falsehood and evil. Wisdom is always disposed to do only good, and she cannot be outwitted by anyone.

The Spirit of God's holy love is always irresistible, beneficent and loving to man. The same may be said of Wisdom for she receives her energies from God's Spirit. Therefore, Wisdom cannot be subdued. She is incapable of producing anything that it not good. Coming forth from the depths of the heart of God, how could Wisdom be anything but loving to man?

The Holy Spirit in Wisdom is steadfast, dependable and always unperturbed. The Wisdom of God, therefore, is not subject to change. She never becomes upset, disturbed or confused. We can always depend upon her for she is perfectly reliable at all times. In attributing to Wisdom those qualities which are exclusively divine, the author emphasizes the divine character of Wisdom.

Wisdom and Creation

In the later Wisdom Literature the writers reveal the origin of Wisdom. They describe the active part she plays in the creation of the universe and show how she leads people to God. The creation account in the Book of Genesis portrays God in the act of creating at the beginning of time. However, when we turn to the Book of Proverbs, we find the sage portraying God as He is eternally, even before the beginning of time. In reflecting on relevant passages in this book as well as in the Book of Sirach, we become aware of the tremendous disclosures about God's inner life of love and the mystery of grace.

The writer of *Proverbs* shows that Wisdom was already in existence at the beginning of time and was present with God at the creation of the world. In personifying Wisdom as a woman, he aptly shows that Wisdom is transcendent, divine and equal to God. His highly descriptive language is both beautiful and compelling as He speaks of the divine origin of Wisdom, her role in creation and her function in the universe. He tells us that Wisdom was there with God when

He "fixed the heavens firm," "assigned the sea its boundaries" and "laid bare the foundations of the earth":

> From everlasting I was firmly set,
>   from the beginning,
>   before earth came into being.
> The deep was not, when I was born,
>   there were no springs to gush with water.
> Before the mountains were settled,
>   before the hills, I came to birth;
>   before he made the earth,
>   the countryside,
>   or the first grains of the world's dust
> (Proverbs 8:23-26).

Wisdom, however, was present with God not only when He created, but she had a role to play in the very act of creating. She was God's "mastercraftsman" as it were. It was Wisdom who drew up the blueprint of the universe:

> I was by his side, a master craftsman,
>   delighting him day after day,
>   ever at play in his presence,
>   at play everywhere in his world,
>   delighting to be with the sons of men
> (Proverbs 8:30-31).

The implication is that Wisdom is the "thought-life," the *Logos* of God, Who knows all that there is to know. Wisdom, was, therefore, necessarily in existence before God created because He had to know what He would do before He did it. Poetically, Wisdom is pictured standing at God's right side when the world was made, furnishing Him with the plan for the creation of all things: "I was by his side, a master craftsman."

The writer then proceeds to reveal the intimate relationship between Wisdom and God. He represents her as God's child "delighting him day after day ever at play in his presence." Wisdom also has a function in the universe and seems to be "at home" with the members of the human race. She is "at play everywhere in his world, delighting to be with the sons of men."

The above passage indicates that the writer of Proverbs had some notion about the plurality of Persons in God, although a distinction of three Persons was not yet manifested. A child "ever at play in his presence" seems to point to the pre-existing Word, the Son of God Who took on human flesh and became a member of the human race when He was born of Mary.

Communication of Wisdom

The author of the Book of Sirach was a scholar, a teacher and a deeply spiritual person.

His contribution to Wisdom Literature was made between 200 and 175 B.C. His writings reveal that Wisdom originates in God and comes from Him alone. This sage is aware of the uniqueness and sublimity of God. He sees Wisdom as an attribute of God which He Himself pours out into creation and gives to "those who love him."

In Chapter Twenty-Four the author gives a masterful discourse in which he has Wisdom speaking for herself. Obviously, he was concerned about the divine communication of Wisdom. He probably was searching for an answer to a question such as, "In what way, precisely, is divine Wisdom directly communicated?"

Ben Sira, a reflective person with a listening heart, received an answer to his question. God communicates His Wisdom beyond the Godhead into the universe through His Word and His Spirit. The energies of His love are locked in His longing thoughts to communicate His presence beyond the Godhead. His Spirit of Love is the power which generates these thoughts and brings them into existence in the universe when He speaks His Word.

Having shown that Wisdom pre-exists with God and comes forth from Him in the work of creation, the sage proceeds to represent Wisdom as the Word coming forth from God in the act of

creating and the Spirit hovering over the waters
at the time of creation:

> *I came forth from the mouth of the Most High,*
> *and I covered the earth like a mist* (Eccle-
> siasticus 24:3).

Reflection

The prologue in John's Gospel might be called
a statement of love, for there we learn of the
everlasting love of the Father. It may be said that
no other writing in history transmits such awe-
some information as that found in this inspiring
hymn, for in this sublime writing the author
deals with the divine origin of Jesus. The theology of presence through the Word-Wisdom of
God that ripened in the Wisdom Literature of
the Old Testament comes to maturity in the Prologue and is developed even more precisely
throughout John's Gospel.

John begins his writings by proceeding to
show that Jesus is truly the creative Word Who
already existed at the beginning of time. Unlike
created things, the pre-existing Word, the *Logos*
of God, was with Him eternally. There never
was a time when God was without His Word-
Wisdom. The evangelist goes so far as to identify
the pre-existing Word with God Himself:

In the beginning was the Word:
the Word was with God
and the Word was God (John 1:1).

In verse 14 John reaches the climax of his hymn. Here he identifies the Word that created the universe with Jesus of Nazareth:

The Word was made flesh,
he lived among us, . . . (John 1:14).

The Word is no longer a presence unseen as in the Tent and the Temple. Nor is the Word merely the presence of divine Wisdom in the Mosaic Law. In the person of Jesus Christ the divine and gracious character of the eternal and invisible God is now seen by men and women. This is the tremendous mystery of the Incarnation by which the Eternal Word took on our exact human nature, becoming one with us in everything except sin.

Now we have the Word of God, not only one with the Father in the Holy Spirit, but also one with human nature. The Eternal Word of God, Who is the perfect Image of the Father, took on human nature by being born of a human mother like every other child. The birth of Jesus made God personally present in the midst of His people.

In the Prologue John describes the "welcome" that the Word-Made-Flesh received when He entered human history:

He was in the world
  that had its being through him,
  and the world did not know him.
He came to his own domain
  and his own people did not accept him
                              (John 1:10-11).

Life was full and interesting without Him. Or perhaps He was too lowly, simple and humble for them. Maybe they were just too busy. Or was it because His thinking did not jibe with theirs? Some probably wanted to follow Him but found it too difficult to "let go" of their comfortable life-style. Consequently, they rationalized away or watered down His teaching so that they might gratify their desires with a "clear" conscience. At any rate, Jesus of Nazareth did not top their list of priorities. Many reasons could be given why the people of His day, and of our day, too, either reject Him altogether or accept Him on their own conditions.

In the next lines John points out that Jesus, however, was not rejected by everyone. Some people did accept Him in His day. There are people who accept Him today. John explains this in his typically beautiful and clear expression. Those who believe in His divine origin share in the same divine "lifestream" that He shares in:

> *But to all who did accept him*
>   *he gave power to become children of God,*
>   *to all who believe in the name of him*
>   *who was born not out of human stock*
>   *or urge of the flesh*
>   *or will of men*
>   *but of God Himself* (John 1:12-13).

The sacred writer tells us that in the person of Jesus Christ the power and wisdom generated by the Father's Holy Spirit of Love are communicated to us. He tells us that the abundance of these riches is never exhausted but is continually bestowed upon us according to our receptivity:

> *Indeed, from his fullness we have,*
>   *all of us, received —*
>   *yes, grace in return for grace* (John 1:16).

The interior flow of grace is from none other than Christ Himself, Whose humanity in union with divinity has the power to draw us into the realm of divine life and love to the degree that we allow Him to do this. The abundance of God's Self-communication to us in His un-created energies of love is never exhausted but is continually renewed according to our need and our availability.

The mission of the Son into the world is to perform the task of making us sons and daughters of the Father by allowing us to share in the love-life of the Trinity. As Christians we share in the same riches Christ shares in as Son of the Father.

8

Wisdom and Divine Self-Communication

The theme of God's Self-communication beyond the Trinity reaches new depths in the Book of Wisdom. About one hundred years before the birth of Jesus a deeply spiritual and learned Jewish writer was given new insights into God's inner life of love. A typical sage of Israel, the author of Wisdom wrote for his fellow Jews whose faith was being shaken by a cultural impact which drew them away from Yahweh.

This writer shows that Wisdom, the *Logos* of God, shares in His divine nature by attributing to her the omnipresence, omnipotence and omniscience of God Himself. He saw in the Word-Wisdom of God those activities and operations which are characteristic of the Word and the Spirit. However, like the authors of *Proverbs* and *Sirach*, the writer of the Book of Wisdom did not present Wisdom as a distinct personality in the Godhead. The theology of three distinct Persons in the Trinity developed only later on in the New Testament writings.

Omnipresence of Wisdom

The God of the Bible is incomprehensible and inaccessible in His essence. Yet, He is not isolated from the world by the perfection of His divine Being. On the contrary, He is present and active in the universe in manifold ways through His uncreated energies of love.

The omnipresence of Wisdom is revealed and praised highly in Chapter Seven of the Book of Wisdom. In speaking of the Spirit in Wisdom the author proclaims her to be almighty and all-surveying. Wisdom is in full possession of God's dynamic and energizing Spirit of Love. She has absolute power over the universe because God's Holy Spirit is in her.

Wisdom makes one uninterrupted survey of every thought in every human heart and she appraises every event and every situation in human history. Through the power of God's Spirit of Love, the Wisdom of God penetrates all human and angelic spirits, making them intelligent, pure and most subtle. In ascribing almighty and all-surveying powers to Wisdom, the writer credits her with presence in angelic and human beings. The Spirit in Wisdom is:

> *almighty, all-surveying*
> *penetrating all intelligent,*
> *pure and most subtle spirits* (Wisdom 7:23).

The sage proceeds to speak of the "mobility" of Wisdom. He seems to imply that Wisdom does not have to move from one place to another because she is already there:

> *Wisdom is quicker to move than any motion;*
> *she is so pure,*
> *she pervades and permeates all things*
> (Wisdom 7:24).

The amazing omnipresence of God's Wisdom means that the vast potential of energy coming from the Holy Spirit of Love is packed in every invisible atom of all matter, for she pervades and permeates all things. Yet, though Wisdom is present in all created reality, she herself remains unhampered because she is unchangeable. Her all-pervading presence and activity cannot be hindered:

> *Although alone, she can do all;*
> *herself unchanging,*
> *she makes all things new* (Wisdom 7:27).

The sacred writer also proclaims that the Spirit in Wisdom is present in human hearts.

The holiness of Wisdom and her immunity to change are qualities which belong to God alone:

In each generation she passes into holy souls,
she makes them friends of God and prophets;
for God loves only the man
who lives with Wisdom (Wisdom 7:27-28).

In communicating to human nature His own essential energy to love and to be loved, God has given each one of us potential for His divine Being. This means that He has given us the potential to share in His own divine nature. It is in the possession of this gift that we are made according to His image and likeness. This potential for His presence is inherent in human nature for it is passed on from generation to generation.

Our potential for God is energized and we are made holy by opening our hearts to receive the communication of divine Wisdom, for God loves those who love her and ask for her. It is through the communication of His Wisdom to us that He makes Himself present to us. When He acts through His Wisdom, He at the same time acts through His Spirit, for the Spirit is the creative and life-giving power in His Wisdom. Therefore, it is one and the same thing to receive Wisdom and to be docile to the Holy Spirit.

Omnipotence of Wisdom

After attributing to Wisdom the omnipresence of God Himself, the author of the Book of Wisdom uses powerful imagery to show that she is omnipotent. He points out that Wisdom originates in God and shares fully in what God Himself is:

She is a breath of the power of God,
pure emanation of the glory of the Almighty;
hence nothing impure can find a way into her
(Wisdom 7:25).

In the act of creating, Wisdom came forth from the depths of God as the blast of creative and life-giving breath. She is the fullness of His power and the glow of His glory. Nothing created can mar the radiant beauty and holiness of His uncreated energies of love.

The sacred writer then depicts Wisdom as the spotless mirror which reflects completely and perfectly the light which is God Himself. The writer tells us that Wisdom images God's goodness with His own expertise:

She is a reflection of the eternal light,
untarnished mirror of God's active power,
image of his goodness (Wisdom 7:26).

The author sees Wisdom coming forth from God as an incomparable light. Created light "must yield to night" but the brilliant light of Wisdom cannot be dimmed by the power of darkness:

> She is indeed more splendid than the sun,
>   she outshines all the constellations;
>   compared with light, she takes first place,
>   for light must yield to night,
>   but over Wisdom evil can never triumph
>   (Wisdom 7:29-30).

Wisdom is not only active in creating the universe, but her power also sustains and governs it. She is, in fact, the providence which directs history. She is associated with all that God does in the world:

> She deploys her strength
>   from one end of the earth to the other,
>   ordering all things for good (Wisdom 8:1).

Omniscience of Wisdom

Love seeks presence but divine intimacy demands oneness. The author of the Book of Wisdom sees Wisdom so one with God that she is in full possession of the infinite knowledge that He Himself possesses eternally. Indeed, she is the thought-life of God Himself. Wisdom, therefore, is omniscient and God allows her to choose what His works should be:

Her closeness to God lends lustre
  to her noble birth,
  since the Lord of All has loved her.
Yes, she is an initiate
  in the mysteries of God's knowledge,
  making choice of the works he is to do
                              (Wisdom 8:3-4).

Wisdom is sent forth from God that she might assume full responsibility for people on earth. Her mission is to bring the thoughts of God to the human race by communicating to people the divine desires, aspirations, attitudes and values which are generated eternally in the heart of God. Intimacy with Wisdom, therefore, is nothing other than intimacy with God Himself.

Divine Self-Communication

In the Old Testament the personal Word-Wisdom had been hidden in God, although it governed the universe, guided history and was manifested in the Law and in the teachings of the sages and prophets. In the New Testament the Word-Wisdom is communicated in fullness to Jesus Christ. United to Christ, we as Christians participate in divine Wisdom and are introduced into the intimacy of the inner life of the Trinity.

The theme of Wisdom as divine Self-communication is an important theological development in the Wisdom Literature. However, while the sages contemplated Wisdom as being in union with God and yet distinct from Him, they gave no clear indication about three Persons in the "God of their Fathers."

The insights of the sages, however, did prove to be of the greatest significance in paving the way for the theology of the Trinity which unfolded in the New Testament. The characteristics applied to Wisdom in the Old Testament were applied to Jesus of Nazareth: "in union with God and at the same time distinct from Him." Indeed, St. Paul points out that the supreme communication of Wisdom came in the Person of Jesus Christ Whom he calls the "Wisdom of God" (I Corinthians 1:24).

Reflection

In the Prologue to his Gospel, John identifies the Word that created the universe and sustains and governs it with Jesus Christ, a member of the human race. John and others had seen and touched Jesus. They saw the beauty and glory of God in His gracious ways and radiant countenance. They saw the divine energies operative in His fearless exposure of the evil of His day as well as in all of His deeds of power and love, for the power and glory of divinity now shone through frail humanity:

> *. . . and we saw his glory,*
> *the glory that is his*
> *as the only Son of the Father*
> *full of grace and truth* (John 1:14).

The power and glory of Jesus are a manifestation of God's presence. His sublime teachings are the light of God's own truth which dispel the darkness of evil in the world. God is now present in the midst of His people in the person of Jesus Christ communicating the Word of the Father. The resurrection of Jesus would finally transform His humanity into the glory of God "full of grace and truth."

In his Prologue John likewise gives emphasis to the nature of life and its origin. It is through His Word that the pre-existing universe in the thoughts of God became created reality. It is through His Word that He imparted to it His own divine energies of life and light. John sees the relationship between life and light. To him, life means sharing in the very Being of God, in the inner love-life of the Father, the Son and the Spirit.

In the physical world light is a precious gift. It lights our way by dispelling darkness. When we are in a dark room, we are fearful of stumbling over objects. However, when we are in a lighted room, we move with assurance. Moreover, light does not only dispel darkness, it also gives life. A plant flourishes and grows in the light of the sun.

John transfers the idea of light overcoming darkness and giving life to the spiritual world. When the light of the Word illuminates the human heart, it enlightens and communicates divine life to us. Not only does it empower us to discern falsehood from truth, but it also communicates divine life by transmitting to us the uncreated energies of power and wisdom and glory inherent in God Himself.

In verse 9 of the Prologue John speaks of the Word as being the true light. The Word Who dwells in light inaccessible to us is going to come into the world so that uncreated light might become available to us:

> The Word was the true light
> that enlightens all men;
> and he was coming into the world (John 1:9).

By "true light" John means the light of the divine order as distinguished from the deception, illusion and darkness present in the human order. The Word is a light that demands a choice. We can choose to allow the Word to become the light of God's presence in our lives, or we can remain in the darkness of our own self-love. When we accept Jesus as Light, we live in Him and He lives in us. Then God Himself becomes present in the words we speak and the actions we perform in our daily situations.

John ends his beautiful hymn by stating that it is Jesus Christ alone Who knows the infinite mystery of God in all fullness. He has come to earth not just to tell us about the Father's love, but to draw us into the infinite riches of His love. It is through the Son that we come to know the Father. The biblical meaning of "know" means to share at the deepest level possible through mutual self-giving:

> *No one has ever seen God;*
> *it is the only Son,*
> *who is nearest to the Father's heart,*
> *who has made him known* (John 1:18).

9

Jesus and the Spirit

The Hebrew people had an exceptionally well-integrated view of life. Not only did they see the "Spirit of Yahweh" as the presence of God's power in all created reality, but they were very conscious of the activity of the Spirit over their own personal lives.

In pondering the writings of the Old Testament, we note that the Hebrews attributed all the energies in the universe such as the power of wind, the force of water, and the heat of the sun to the Spirit of God. They also attributed to the Spirit of God all human energies. For example, the speed of athletes, the skill of craftsmen, the wisdom of sages and the insights of prophets emanated from God's own energies of love. For the Hebrew, then, the Spirit was the power of God Himself present and active in the universe and the lives of people.

The Spirit of God

For many centuries the Israelites had waited for the coming of the promised Messiah. They longed for a true king, a man in whom God's Spirit would become active. They saw in their future king an energetic and vigorous person whose leadership would flow out of the power and wisdom imparted to him by the Spirit of God. They knew their need for someone who would help them to strengthen their covenant relationship to the God of their Fathers.

The prophet Isaiah described in some detail the distinguishing and striking qualities of the long-awaited Messiah. He emphasized the activity of the Spirit in their future king. He saw the Spirit of God as the life-giving "breath" that would come from Yahweh to their savior-king. Thus, their future leader would be endowed with extraordinary powers. Indeed, he would be someone filled with the spirit of their ancestors, for their ideal king would have the wisdom of Solomon and the courage, prudence and leadership of David. He would also have the knowledge and fear of the Lord which was characteristic of the patriarchs and prophets:

A shoot springs from the stock of Jesse,
a scion thrusts from his roots:
on him the spirit of Yahweh rests,
a spirit of wisdom and insight,
a spirit of counsel and power,
a spirit of knowledge
   and of the fear of Yahweh (Isaiah 11:1-2).

As we read the New Testament we find the Spirit of God in close association with Jesus. Saint Luke reveals in his Gospel that the Spirit of God was active in the life of Jesus from the very beginning. When the All-Powerful Word of God leaped from the heart of the Father and took on human flesh in the womb of Mary, the Spirit of God was present. Although Mary was a virgin, the angel assured her that she would bear a child Who would be conceived by the power of the Holy Spirit:

"The Holy Spirit will come upon you"
   the angel answered
"and the power of the Most High
   will cover you with its shadow"

(Luke 1:35).

Jesus was not only conceived by the power of God's Spirit, but He was baptized and anointed for His mission by the Spirit. He was driven into the desert by the Spirit of God, and He healed, performed miracles and cast out demons by the power of the Spirit.

The New Testament goes on to reveal that not only did Jesus receive the Spirit Himself, but He sent the Holy Spirit to His followers. However, He could not communicate the Spirit of God to others until His own humanity had been transformed and glorified by the Holy Spirit in His resurrection.

The Beloved Son

The Gospels tell us that the mission of John the Baptist was to prepare the people for the coming of the "ideal king" who would inaugurate the kingdom of God. The people who accepted John's call to baptism were in earnest about turning away from their former pretentious and self-centered life-style and committing themselves to a new and more genuine spirituality.

Such a change in one's life would involve a close examination of personal priorities. It called for a "metanoia," a change of heart which is an uprooting of selfish attitudes and false values. Those who accepted John's baptism indicated their willingness to undergo a change of heart in order to become a member of the imminent "kingdom" that John was so emphatically proclaiming.

In response to the call coming from John to

undergo a baptism of repentance, Jesus emerged from the obscurity of His hidden life in Nazareth and went down to the waters of the Jordan. In His decision to accept the baptism of John, Jesus made the human choice to embrace the vocation given Him by His Father. Here at the Jordan He publicly accepted His messianic role of redeeming the human race according to the loving plan of His Father.

The observant John notices Jesus standing in line waiting His turn to be baptized. There He stood among sinners, silently demonstrating His solidarity with the guilt and brokenness of the whole human race. He Himself needed no repentance, no change of heart. But in His decision to be baptized, He freely submitted to the will of His Father and humbly placed Himself in the midst of sinners.

The baptism of Jesus by John is crowned by the Holy Spirit descending on Him. The same Spirit Who was sent forth by God to hover over the waters at the first creation now hovered over the waters of the Jordan at the beginning of a new creation. In the Old Testament imagery, the dove is the symbol of love. In the baptism of Jesus, the Spirit of Love is represented by the dove. Luke mentions that Jesus was praying privately when the Holy Spirit came upon Him:

Now when all the people had been baptized
and while Jesus after his own baptism
was at prayer, heaven opened
and the Holy Spirit descended on him
in bodily shape, like a dove

(Luke 3:21-22).

Centuries earlier Isaiah had depicted the true king, the expected human savior, as the great servant of God. He pictured him as someone who would be most pleasing to God:

Here is my servant whom I uphold,
my chosen one in whom my soul delights.
I have endowed him with my spirit
that he may bring true justice to the nations

(Israel 42:1).

At the baptism of Jesus the Heavenly Father openly expressed His love for the One Who gives Him delight. At the moment when Jesus fully accepted His messianic role by being baptized as a sinner, the Father acknowledged His great pleasure over His Son's free choice:

And a voice came from heaven,
"You are my Son, the Beloved;
my favor rests on you" (Luke 3:22).

Here we find the Father accepting the deliberate and free Self-gift of this man Jesus, Who is pledging Himself to be the kind of Messiah the Father wants Him to be. Freely and without any reservations, Jesus accepted the role of the suffering servant. It is His mission to bring to the broken human race the redemptive and healing love of the Father. He is the One through Whom God will bring about the redemption of all people.

Jesus, Fully Human

After His baptism Jesus was led by the Spirit of God into the wilderness to be tempted:

Filled with the Holy Spirit,
Jesus left the Jordan
and was led by the Spirit through the
*   wilderness,*
being tempted there by the devil
for forty days (Luke 4:1-2).

The temptation experiences in the desert make it clear that Jesus was fully human. His human choice to reject them show His full intent to be the kind of Messiah that the Father had in mind for Him.

Because of the fasting that Jesus imposed upon Himself while in the desert, He became very hungry. Aware of His human need for food, the tempter tried to induce Jesus to turn stones into bread. After all, if He really were the Son of

God, He should be able to do this.

But Jesus was not deceived by the subtlety of Satan. He recognized this experience as a temptation to exercise His messianic power for His own personal advantage. But Jesus knew that He was to use these powers to dispel the darkness of sin and illusion in peoples' lives and to heal their brokenness by communicating to them the Word of God. So Jesus replied:

> *"Man does not live on bread alone*
> *but on every word*
> *that comes from the mouth of God"*
> (Matthew 4:4).

In resisting the temptation to misuse His divine powers, Jesus demonstrated His obedience to His Father's will for Him. In this temptation Jesus overcame any desire He might have had to act independently of His Father from Whom He had received everything. In the incident in the desert and in every temptation in His public ministry, Jesus refused to operate outside of His Father's will for Him.

In the second temptation Jesus was tempted to throw Himself off the temple parapet. If He were truly the Son of God, He would surely be saved by divine power! Such an action would certainly draw a crowd and would guarantee belief in Him. But Jesus rejected the temptation to "show off" His messianic powers to make an impression on others. Once again He quoted Scripture:

"You must not put the Lord your God
to the test" (Matthew 4:7).

In the final temptation in the desert, Satan revealed himself as the ruler of the kingdom of darkness. He tried to dissuade Jesus from living out His Suffering Servant role by offering Him worldly riches, honor and power. Jesus was tempted to become a political Messiah so that He might enjoy the accompanying prestige, power and glory. But Jesus flatly refused the offer:

"Be off, Satan! . . .
You must worship the Lord your God,
and serve him alone" (Matthew 4:10).

The temptations in the desert show that Jesus was fully human. They are indicative of the temptations He later experienced during His public ministry. Again and again Jesus was tempted to impose on His Father His own way of living out His Messiahship. Like us, He had to make a human choice for He was free to say yes or no to every temptation. But in every instance He chose to remain dependent on His Father in humility and loving obedience. It is no wonder that He was so precious to His Father Who took delight in His Son!

Up to the very end of His life Jesus suffered from temptation. Even in the Garden of Gethsemane He was tempted to use His divine powers to save Himself. He was tempted to flee. But because He accepted His Father's will, "Let your will be done, not mine," Jesus found Himself yielding in perfect surrender and obedience. He surrendered out of love for His Father Whom He longed to please and out of love for us whom He longed to redeem.

On the Cross, Jesus experienced the most painful temptation of all when He momentarily doubted His Father's love for Him. He felt abandoned by His beloved Father to Whom He had given such perfect obedience all during His lifetime. It was not easy for Him to hear the words of the scoffers, "If you are God's Son, come down from the cross." He could still have used His divine power to His own advantage, but He refused to do so. As always, Jesus prayed when He was tempted. When He uttered His last words, "Father, into your hands I commit my Spirit," His temptations ended.

Up to the very last moment of His life Jesus had been tempted to supplant His Father's redemptive plan with His own. He struggled with temptation as long as He lived just as we struggle with it. He overcame it by surrendering to the Father in faith and loving obedience just as we overcome it.

Reflection

Jesus grew in human freedom through His continued surrender to His Father. He exercised His freedom by pleasing His Father in every aspect of His daily life situations. In contemplating His Father's love for Him, He always responded to that love by abandoning His own way of living out His Messiahship and following perfectly the will of His Father. In spite of pain, rejection and the human dread of a horrible death, Jesus always maintained absolute trust in the Father's love for Him.

New Testament writings reveal that faith in Jesus Christ is the source of our spiritual life. The greatest temptation that we must undergo all through our lives is the test to die to self-love by abandoning ourselves in absolute trust to Christ's love for us. To the degree that we abandon ourselves to Him in faith, to that degree does Jesus Christ become the power of God in our lives.

A real faith in Christ must be more than mere acquiescence to the story of Jesus with its social, moral and spiritual implications. It requires more than an attempt to imitate His humility, His compassion, His loving service and His other virtues. It must be more than merely living out His more palatable teachings. The true dimension of faith in Jesus Christ calls for something more than all of this.

If our faith in Jesus Christ is real, we will rely on Him in complete abandonment knowing that He will take care of us even though we may not see how He intends to do so. Furthermore, we will be willing to "let go" of anything in our lives which may prevent us from developing a personal relationship to Him. It is in this kind of fidelity to Him that the Holy Spirit works within us, transforming our way of thinking and our way of loving at profound depths. It lies within our freedom to desire this kind of faith. It is up to us to accept it rather than reject it.

We must allow our faith in Jesus to grow amid struggle, temptations and sufferings. It must be allowed to mature in times of doubt and darkness. The more we identify with Christ in our "Yes, Father" in the acceptance of ourselves and the happenings of each day, the more do we accept His presence in our lives. True Christian acceptance of Christ's presence in our lies means to realize that God will be faithful to us in every situation. This kind of faith gives us an inner vision whereby we begin to see the loving activity of God operating in our lives. It gives us great sensitivity to His wishes for us in our daily human endeavors and encounters.

As our faith in Jesus Christ matures, we are gradually freed of compulsive desires, cleansed of anger and less disturbed by fear of what others may think or say. As we abandon ourselves to Him at deeper levels, we are less drawn by the norms of a "worldly" society and less influenced by popular ideologies which may run counter to the teachings of Christ and His Church. As our hearts become more free, our relationship to Jesus becomes more personal. His presence becomes less nebulous and more real. He becomes Someone to us.

The faith that Jesus Christ desires of us then, is the kind that removes the fear of allowing Him to take over in our lives. This calls for an on-going act of self-abandonment whereby we no longer rely merely on our own human way of looking at reality, but open ourselves to the Wisdom and the Power of Him in Whom we believe. Being "in touch" with Christ in faith empowers us to overcome our temptations. This enables us to participate ever more fully in His great redemptive work of helping to transform the world by freeing people from the forces of evil.

10

Jesus and the Father

The Holy Spirit Whom Jesus had received at baptism became the dominating power in His whole ministry. Enlightened by the Spirit of God, Jesus came to understand that His mission would be to fulfill the Old Testament prophecies regarding the "ideal king."

After being tempted in the desert, Jesus returned to Galilee and began to teach the people. His reputation as a teacher spread rapidly through the countryside. On one occasion when He was in His hometown of Nazareth, He went to the synagogue on the Sabbath. While there, someone handed Him the scroll of the prophet Isaiah. He unrolled it and read:

The spirit of the Lord has been given to me,
for he has anointed me.
He has sent me

to bring the good news to the poor,
to proclaim liberty to captives
and to the blind new sight,
to set the downtrodden free,
to proclaim the Lord's year of favour
                                        (Luke 4:18-19).

After the reading Jesus rolled up the scroll, gave it back to the assistant and sat down. He now fully realized that the whole thrust of His ministry would be to release people from the forces of evil. So He said to the people in the synagogue:

"This text is being fulfilled today
even as you listen" (Luke 4:21).

Jesus Served

Though alienated from God, the world itself is not evil. All of creation is good. In a special way every human being since the time of Adam has been the object of God's loving concern and compassion. In the fourth Gospel, John stresses the graciousness of the Father's love and shows that it is the Father's passionate desire that not one person should perish. That is precisely why He sent His beloved Son into the world:

Yes, God loved the world so much
that he gave his only Son,

so that everyone who believes in him
may not be lost
but may have eternal life (John 3:16).

Because God is love, He seeks to share the presence of Himself. Jesus did everything He could do to share His presence with others. He taught them and served them in every way possible. But the service that He rendered always flowed out of His prayer. Indeed, Jesus was a contemplative in action because everything that He said and did was a sharing of His contemplative union with the Father.

In the fourth Gospel we find the amazing revelation that the Father not only loves the Son but has handed everything over to Him. For instance, Jesus does not teach on His own initiative but everything that He says comes from His shared knowledge with the Father:

"My teaching is not from myself:
it comes from the one who sent me"
(John 7:16).

In order to communicate His thoughts to us, the Father speaks through His Son Jesus. Therefore, Jesus conveys only what He has received from the Father. He does this so that we will come to know the "thinking" of the Father and grow in divine Wisdom. As we grow in Wisdom, we come to know not only how the Father wishes us to live, but we also become more conscious of the immense love that the Father has for each one of us.

If we ponder the many discourses of Jesus in John's Gospel, we will notice how freely Jesus talks about the relationship between Himself and the Father. He does not hesitate to tell the people that He refuses to operate independently of the Father. On the other hand, He very openly explains that He depends on the Father as the Source of all that He is and does.

Obviously, there is absolute accord between Father and Son because Jesus does not seek glory for Himself. He is in the world to do the work of the Father — and only the work of the Father. Love is the principle of this communion of activity between Father and Son just as love is the principle of the activity of the Spirit. All the deeds of power and love of Jesus demand an identity of nature, a mutual sharing of infinite power and knowledge:

> "I tell you most solemnly,
> the Son can do nothing by himself;
> he can do only what he sees the Father doing:
> and whatever the Father does
> the Son does too" (John 5:19).

The preaching of Jesus had a great impact on the people who heard Him. Like John the Baptist, He preached repentance — the kind of repentance which involves conversion of heart. He called for a turning away from preoccupation with self and earthly realities because it is this that makes people available to His redemptive activity. In such conversion, rationalizations cease and the compromise of Christian values discontinues.

Jesus also preached the good news of His Father's infinite love and mercy for each person and how each one should respond to the Father's love. The Father's compassion for individuals was conveyed to them through Jesus. He had a burning desire to lead people to respond to the Father's love for them. Through His whole public life, He went about doing good, serving people with the intent of reconciling them to God and to one another. His loving service of preaching and doing good ended when He gave up His life in the ultimate Gift of Himself to His Father for human society.

Jesus Prayed

Being one with the Father, Jesus was filled with the Father's holy love. From the Gospels we learn that Jesus often prayed alone before His Father — sometimes through the entire night. But He also prayed when His apostles and other people were around.

Jesus prayed at His baptism, and when He was tempted in the desert. He prayed when He raised Lazarus from the dead, and when He was prostrate in the garden in Gethsemane. Jesus prayed, too, when He was hanging on the cross. In all of His prayer, Jesus was one with His Father in total surrender of Self to Him.

It is in the setting of the Last Supper that we see Jesus as a man of deep prayer. In this situation the heart of Jesus speaks out to the Father with great intensity. When Jesus was nearing the hour of His death, He wanted to have one last meal with His apostles, His closest friends. From the manner in which He conducted Himself during this farewell gathering, we can sense the depth of His holy love for His Father and for all humankind.

The atmosphere in the Supper Room was charged with apprehension. The apostles were puzzled by the washing of feet and they were disturbed by the mention of betrayal. Peter especially was upset. He really loved Jesus. Yet, Jesus had intimated that Peter would deny Him. All were depressed and anxious because Jesus was talking about leaving them.

The same love that is at the root of the relationship between Father and Son is also at the root of the relationship between Jesus and the apostles. Knowing what was in their hearts and sensitive to their feelings, Jesus pleaded with these friends not to lose faith in Him:

> *"Do not let your hearts be troubled,*
> *Trust in God still, and trust in me"*
>
> (John 14:1-2).

The so-called priestly prayer of Jesus which is recorded in John's Gospel reveals His great concern for His disciples and for all people. Overcome by the Father's tender love for Him and in gratitude for His loving care throughout the challenging period of His public ministry, Jesus entered into prayerful communion with His Father during the meal. With deep feeling He prayed:

> *"Father, the hour has come:*
> *glorifly your Son*
> *so that your Son may glorify you;*
> *and, through the power over all mankind*
> *that you have given him,*
> *let him give eternal life*
> *to all those you have entrusted to him"*
>
> (John 17:1-2).

Jesus had glorified His Father by communicating His presence to others through all the words and deeds of His life. Now the Father will glorify Jesus by having Him return to the original glory He shared with Him eternally.

The purpose of Jesus' sojourn in the world was to make available to the human race the inner love-life of the Trinity. These men who were gathered together with Him during this meal were to be key people in helping to carry out the divine plan.

Though often lacking in understanding, the apostles were faithful to the teaching given them by Jesus. Aware of the divine responsibility that would be theirs in continuing His redemptive work, Jesus interceded with the Father in their behalf. He knew that they would need divine guidance and protection. So He prayed:

> *"I pray for them;*
> *I am not praying for the world*
> *but for those you have given me,*
> *because they belong to you"* (John 17:9).

While praying to His Father, Jesus thought of the Church. He wanted it to have a spiritual impact in the world. His Church was to continue through the ages, remaining unaffected by worldly values. Jesus knew that the world would hate the truth which would be communicated through His Church.

Since the apostolic mission of the Church is the same as Christ's mission from the Father, the Church would become the divine-human instrument for communicating the power and wisdom of the inner love-life of the Trinity. So Jesus addressed His Father in behalf of all future people who would believe in Him by accepting the testimony passed on by the disciples:

"I pray not only for these,
but for those also
who through their words
will believe in me" (John 17:20).

Jesus included in His prayer, then, a plea that the work begun by Him would reach completion. He wanted His work of bringing the transforming love of the Father to human beings to go on even after His physical departure from earth. It was through His Church that the love He received from His Father would be passed on to others.

Jesus Loved

Before the Incarnation, the Son of God shared fully in the glory of the power and knowledge of the Father. His love for us, however, was so deep that He willingly "let go" of His divine glory and became one of us. Jesus was a very ordinary person. He knew the inconveniences of inclement weather and the fatigue of hard work. He experienced not only joy and success in His work but also disappointment and rejection.

Jesus had to make all kinds of decisions during His lifetime just as we do. But all of His decisions were made in response to the loving wishes of His Father. Ordinary decisions were made rather spontaneously; more serious ones were the outcome of reflection and deep silent prayer. Not satisfied with simply carrying out the commands of His Father, He sought always to carry out His slightest wish.

However, in His passionate desire to please His Father, Jesus went even beyond the point of carrying out His Father's wishes. He wanted His Self-gift in response to His Father's love to be total. That is why He made the human decision to take upon Himself the guilt of the human race. He reached the peak of speaking His yes to the Father when He gave up His body and His blood while hanging on a cross.

The Son of God had taken on human flesh that He might communicate to us the uncreated energies of God's love. This meant a life of service. But the ultimate service that Jesus rendered to humanity was enacted on Calvary. He was willing to take upon Himself the punishment that the human race brings upon itself through self-imposed alienation from God. His willingness to carry out the redemptive plan of the Father flowed out of His immense love for His Father and us. It is through the death of Jesus that we are saved from everlasting alienation from God. The prophetic description of the sufferings of Jesus is found in Isaiah:

> *And yet ours were the sufferings he bore,*
> *ours the sorrow he carried.*
> *But we, we thought of him as someone*
> *punished,*
> *struck by God, and brought low.*
> *Yet he was pierced through for our faults,*
> *crushed for our sins.*
> *On him lies a punishment that brings us peace,*
> *and through his wounds we are healed*
> (Isaiah 53:4-5).

The Son of God experienced not only horrible physical suffering but also one of the most painful types of human suffering that is possible. He was even rejected by His own. But He suffered all, humbly and quietly — displaying a most unusual silence:

> *Harshly dealt with, he bore it humbly,*
> *he never opened his mouth,*
> *like a lamb that is led to the slaughter-*
> *house,*
> *like a sheep that is dumb before its shearers*
> *never opening its mouth* (Isaiah 53:7).

If the Father manifests His love by allowing His beloved Son to take on human flesh and to be born of Mary in Bethlehem, how much more does He manifest His love for us by allowing this Son to give up His life for sinful humankind:

> *"A man can have no greater love*
> *than to lay down his life*
> *for his friends"* (John 15:13).

Reflection

In the Old Testament, suffering was taken seriously. Profound compassion for the sufferer is found again and again. Bruised by suffering, but carried along by faith in God's love for them, prophets and sages gradually entered into contemplative union with God as they discovered the purifying value of suffering. They learned that suffering is like fire which separates the metal from its impurities.

In the New Testament, Jesus could not witness suffering without being profoundly moved by divine love. When He saw the crowds of broken people before Him, He was moved to pity for they seemed to be lost and aimless like sheep without a shepherd. Yet, Jesus did not suppress suffering, but consoled the one who suffered. He did not abolish tears but dried them.

The gospel approach to suffering is that the Cross is a human reality. Christ Himself teaches us the value of suffering. People can grow bitter through suffering or they can become enriched. When suffering is accepted, people become open, wise, gentle and even transparent. Pain can glorify us, make us radiant and bring fruitfulness to our lives.

If we have not already experienced suffering in our lives, perhaps someday we will face a crisis or be in some stressful situation. It may be the prolonged and agonizing death of someone very dear to us. Or we may experience betrayal when a friend whom we love and to whom we have confided our deepest thoughts and ideals turns and goes another way. This is very painful suffering.

Or again, we may be disappointed in ourselves when suddenly it seems we are not what we always thought we were. In a sense we feel that we are a fraud. Or perhaps we are being grossly misunderstood and our fondest aspirations are coldly ignored. Or there may be the crisis of being told that our labors are in vain and that we are being rated "unsatisfactory." We begin to feel that we ourselves are one big failure.

Such experiences as these can leave us depressed, suspicious, bitter and cynical. Or they can be the means of growth making us even more fruitful and effective in our human endeavors and encounters.

When sorrow overwhelms us, we can either take refuge in self-pity and find compensations in various forms, or we can accept this experience as a personal purification. If we allow Jesus to be Lord in our lives by turning to Him in faith, He will help us to handle any crisis in our life. This is a moment of grace if we accept it.

In all situations of life the will of God comes to us above all as an interior invitation to personal love. But we must come to believe that the love of God seeks our good in every situation. He is trying to dispose us for the great love He wants to share. Therefore, we must gradually open our hearts all the way with absolute faith in His love for us. He Himself has said that He will bring good out of every situation if we allow Him to do so:

> *"I tell you, most solemnly,*
> *unless a grain of wheat*
> *falls on the ground and dies,*
> *it remains only a single grain;*
> *but if it dies,*
> *it yields a rich harvest"* (John 12:24).

This approach to our daily life situations is the genuine life-style of the gospel. In allowing ourselves to be emptied as Christ was emptied, we enter into close communion with Him. To become one with Christ means to accept with gratitude not only the joys of our lives, but also the humiliations, the deprivations, the frustrations and the sufferings of each day. This becomes possible when we really believe that we will be sustained and supported by the immense love of Jesus Who lives in us.

11

A New Presence

All through the Old Testament, the sacred writers reveal that the Word of God and the Spirit never ceased to act together. God communicated the Power and Wisdom of His uncreated energies of love in many ways but especially through the Law and the prophets. The Word of the Law and the words of the prophetic utterances were the means of communicating the thoughts of God, while the Spirit was the gentle transforming power bringing into reality the meaning behind the words.

These two distinct roles of the Word and the Spirit are found also in the New Testament. The Spirit is never without the Word; nor is the Word ever without the Spirit. The Word took on human flesh through the power of the Spirit. Throughout His entire life, Jesus did nothing without the Spirit working in Him. Even since His return to the Father as the Risen Lord, He continues His redemptive work on earth through the Spirit of God's love.

Humanity Glorified

Jesus hardly ever mentioned the Spirit until the evening of the Last Supper. As long as He was with His apostles, He was their Paraclete and Consoler. They felt secure when He was in their midst. That is why the news of His approaching departure upset them so much. At that time, the apostles did not know that the Spirit of Love Who proceeds from the Father and the Son would become their "Spirit" too.

However, Jesus tried to console the apostles by letting them know that He planned to send the Spirit to help them understand the meaning of His mission. The Holy Spirit would lead the apostles to a knowledge of the truths that Jesus Himself brought directly from the Father:

> "I have said these things to you
> while still with you;
> but the Advocate, the Holy Spirit,
> whom the Father will send in my name,
> will teach you everything
> and remind you of all
> I have said to you" (John 14:25-26).

However, the Spirit would not be released to the apostles until the total humanity of Jesus Himself was transformed and divinized by the power of the Spirit. This would happen in the resurrection of Jesus' body. Only then would the Spirit be released and given to other human beings.

From all eternity, the Son enjoyed full glory with the Father. When He took on human flesh, He assumed all the limitations of weak human nature. Thus He surrendered the glory of God's powerful presence within Him in order to become one of us:

> *His state was divine,*
> *yet he did not cling*
> *to his equality with God*
> *but emptied himself*
> *to assume the condition of a slave,*
> *and became as men are;*
> *and being as all men are,*
> *he was humbler yet,*
> *even to accepting death,*
> *death on a cross* (Philippians 2:6-8).

As a human being, Jesus was like us in every way except that He never sinned. He worked hard for a living. He experienced hunger, thirst and fatigue. He grew in human knowledge as we do, and through experience He learned how to cope with the problems of life.

In complete openness to His Father's love, Jesus lived His life in full submission and obedience to His Father's will. He freely accepted the human shame and suffering which accompanied His rejection and death on the Cross. He endured it all for love of us. For this reason, the Father later exalted Him and raised Him to full glory. In the Risen Jesus we have a human being in full possession of the glory of God:

> *But God raised him high*
> *and gave him the name*
> *which is above all other names*
> *so that all beings in the heavens,*
> *on earth and in the underworld,*
> *should bend the knee at the name of Jesus*
> *and that every tongue should acclaim*
> *Jesus Christ as Lord,*
> *to the glory of God the Father*
>
> (Philippians 2:9-11)

It was only in His death and resurrection that Jesus could finally pour out the fullness of His Spirit to others. In rising, Jesus passed over from the corruptible state of limited human nature to the incorruptible divinized state of His humanity. In His glorified humanity He moved into the fullness of a new state of being not only toward the Father but toward every human person.

Now His redeeming power could be extended to all people of all times.

No longer was Jesus hampered by the human limitations which were His during His public ministry. No longer was He restricted to those few people of Palestine because of language, time and space. Transformed fully by the Spirit, Jesus went to His heavenly Father in His glorified humanity, and from there He continues His redemptive work through the power of His Spirit.

Pentecost Event

Centuries before the Pentecost Event, the prophet Joel had promised an outpouring of the Spirit on all mankind. Peter's discourse in Acts 2:16-21 identifies the miracle of Pentecost as the fulfillment of this prophecy. The baptism of the Spirit foretold by John the Baptist was initiated by the outpouring of the Spirit on the disciples of Jesus while they were gathered together in the Upper Room:

When Pentecost day came round, they had all met in one room, when suddenly they heard what sounded like a powerful wind from heaven, the noise of which filled the entire house in which they were sitting; and something appeared to them that seemed like tongues of fire; these separated and came to rest on the head of each of them. They were all filled with the Holy Spirit, and began to speak foreign languages as the Spirit gave them the gift of speech (Acts 2:1-4).

In the Pentecost happening, the Holy Spirit of the Father's love began to flow freely from the glorified body of Jesus into His disciples. The same Spirit of Love Who brings the Father and Son to oneness within the Trinity was now present and active in the hearts of the apostles.

Filled with the Spirit of God's holy love, they went out to the people who had gathered in the streets. Without wasting any time, Peter began to speak with them. No longer was he afraid as he faced some of the crowd who had demanded His Master's death some weeks earlier. Enlightened by the Spirit of the Father and the Son, Peter now understood the meaning behind Christ's teachings, His ministry, death and resurrection. He referred to Jesus as a man given to them by God and Someone through whom God had worked. He had great news for these people, but first of all he confronted them with an embarrassing truth:

This man, who was put into your power by the deliberate intention and foreknowledge of God, you took and had crucified by men out-

side the Law. You killed him, but God raised him to life, . . . (Acts 2:23-24).

Peter's reference to Jesus of Nazareth as a man through whom God had worked and his accusation that they were responsible for His crucifixion pricked the consciences of these people:

Hearing this, they were cut to the heart and said to Peter and the apostles, "What must we do, brothers?" (Acts 2:37).

Peter knew the answer. He insisted on an inner conversion of heart. Then he led them to a desire for baptism so that they might also receive the Spirit of the Risen Lord into their own hearts:

"You must repent," Peter answered "and every one of you must be baptized in the name of Jesus Christ for the forgiveness of your sins, and you will receive the gift of the Holy Spirit" (Acts 2:38).

The Gift of the Spirit, therefore, was not to be for the disciples alone. The sacred writer records that many people were baptized that same day. It was in this new little community of believers, born of the Spirit, that the Church was conceived. Jesus Himself was now present in these people because the Word and the Spirit are inseparable:

Your body, you know,
  is the temple of the Holy Spirit,
  who is in you
  since you received him from God
                    (1 Corinthians 6:19).

Christian Baptism

The greatest work of the Spirit is to lead people to God. The more we grow in union with Him, the more fully do we share in His uncreated energies of power and knowledge. We are initiated into the inner life of the Trinity and begin to share in God's uncreated energies of love in a special way when we are born of the Spirit in the Sacrament of Baptism:

"I tell you most solemnly,
unless a man is born
through water and the Spirit,
he cannot enter the kingdom of God:
what is born of the flesh is flesh;
what is born of the Spirit is spirit" (John 3:5-6).

The natural life communicated to us at the time of our physical birth came from our natural parents. We are their sons and daughters because we share in their life. The spiritual life communicated to us in baptism comes from the Spirit of God. We are sons and daughters of the

Father because we share in His life. This sharing in the life of God through our spiritual birth is every bit as real as our sharing in the life of our parents through our physical birth.

The Spirit is the Love that the Father has for the Son and the Son has for the Father. This Spirit of Love is now actively present in the baptized Christian. Hence, the Holy Spirit does more than simply intercede, admonish and guide. He is the Principle of a new life that is truly divine. He is in us! We grow and mature as true children of the Father through the activity of the Spirit Who leads us out of darkness into the light of Christ.

It is the same Holy Spirit, the bond of love between the Father and the Son in the Trinity, Who comes to us in the Sacrament of Baptism. It is the indwelling Spirit Who puts us in direct contact with the glorified Body of Jesus. Since Jesus is one with the Father, He dwells in us too, because the Trinitarian community can never be separated. Jesus explained this to the apostles when he was with them at the Last Supper:

"If anyone loves me he will keep my word,
and my Father will love him,
and we shall come to him
and make our home with him" (John 14:23).

Eucharistic Presence

It is in the Eucharist that God's uncreated energies of love become most available to us. Jesus Christ, the Eternal Word-Wisdom of the Father, comes to us in the Eucharist with the fullness of divinity shining through His glorified humanity.

Drawn together into oneness with the Father by the Spirit of Love, Jesus is in full possession of the Father's uncreated energies of love. Hence, when we receive the Body and Blood of the glorified humanity of Jesus, we receive also the Father, for the Risen Jesus can never be separated from the Father and Holy Spirit relationships.

When we receive the Body and Blood of Jesus, we are engrafted into the divinized humanity of Jesus just as a branch is inserted into the life-stream of a vine. In His magnificent discourse after He fed the multitude, Jesus taught that the divine life which the Father communicates to Him as His Son, is passed on to us in the Eucharist:

> "He who eats my flesh
>   and drinks my blood
>   lives in me and I live in him.
> As I, who am sent by the living Father,
>   myself draw life from the Father,

> *so whoever eats me*
> *will draw life from me"* (John 6:56-57).

In giving us His own Body and Blood as food and drink in the Eucharist, Jesus shares with us His very own life. Having been initiated into divine life by the Spirit in baptism, it is in the Eucharist that the Holy Spirit progressively brings about our new birth as a child of God.

In the early centuries of the Church, the Eastern Fathers taught that this is a union in the literal sense of the word. It is a true incorporation into Christ's very own substance. Thus, it is in the Eucharist that God makes available to us the unsearchable riches of His uncreated energies of love, the infinite power and knowledge of the Father Himself.

Reflection

According to the teachings of the Eastern Fathers on grace, God does not communicate His essence to us. We are created but He is uncreated. Obviously, it is not possible for limited created beings to share fully in the essence of the unlimited, uncreated God. However, God does make it possible for human beings to participate in His divine nature. He does this by communicating Himself to us in His uncreated energies of love.

Love seeks to share the presence of self. Since God is love, He seeks to share His presence beyond the Godhead. That is why He created.

God created human beings according to His own image and likeness that we might share in the very love-life of the Trinitarian Community: the Father, the Son and the Holy Spirit. However, through the misuse of human freedom in the Garden of Eden, God's loving presence was rejected. At this point, sin and suffering entered into the lives of people because, apart from God, human beings cannot cope with the forces of evil.

Unable to restrain the energies of His love for His suffering children, God longed unceasingly to share His presence with them even though they deliberately had rejected Him. At the time of creation, He had poured forth the uncreated energies of His love into the universe by sending forth His Spirit and His Word. Now, once again, He would send forth the energies of His love through His Spirit and His Word — this time to transform the unholy love which was leading the human race to self-destruction.

In the Old Testament, we have the story of how God communicated His presence to the Israelite people by communicating His Wisdom to them through the Law and the prophets. In the New Testament, God reached the ultimate in Self-communication. The Father Himself did not come to earth in Person, but His Son and His Spirit did. They came precisely to communicate the energies of the Father's love to the human race so that self-centered love might become other-centered, unholy love might become holy.

The mission of the Word-Made-Flesh and the Spirit of God in the world, then, is to transform human love by bringing the healing energies of the Father's love to broken humanity. In doing so, they bring the presence of the Father into our lives. However, the Father does not force His love upon us because love is something that cannot be forced.

On the human level, love seeks union. Union is not possible, however, without mutual consent. The same holds true in our relationship to God. Through His Word, the Father unceasingly offers Himself to us in the Spirit of His Love. He waits for our total surrender to Him.

Healed by divine love, we become ever more conscious of our oneness with the Indwelling Trinity. We grow in the the awareness that we are not alone in coping with our daily life situations. But what is more, we willingly identify with the Suffering Christ in His on-going redemptive work of leading others to the Father's love.